C000230670

MORE *Manchester* MEMORIES

The publishers would like to thank the following companies for their

support in the production of this book

Main Sponsor

Sykes Seafoods Ltd

Bauer Millett & Co Ltd

Desser & Co Ltd

Arthur Gresty Ltd

William Hulme's Grammar School

Kellogg's

R H Lord & Son (Asphalters) Ltd

Manchester Airport Plc

The Manchester Grammar School

Waters MS Technologies Centre / Micromass UK Ltd

Salford Van Hire Ltd

Tenmat Ltd

Voith Paper Ltd

Williams Motor Company

W Wing Yip Plc

First published in Great Britain by True North Books Limited
England HX3 6AE
01422 344344

Copyright © True North Books Limited, 2006

All rights reserved. No part of this publication may be reproduced, stored in a retrieval system, or transmitted in any form, or by any means, electronic, mechanical, photocopy recording or otherwise without the prior permission in writing of the Copyright holders, nor be otherwise circulated in any form or binding or cover other than in which it is published and without a similar condition being imposed on the subsequent publisher.

ISBN 1 903204 89 5

Text, design and origination by True North Books
Printed and bound by The Amadeus Press

MORE *Manchester* MEMORIES

CONTENTS

INTRODUCTION

We have all taken to the road on our travels. Many of us have turned to the air, whilst others use the seas around our island. 'More Manchester Memories' it is an opportunity to indulge in time travel. There is no magical Tardis to transport you back through history, what we have is page after page of nostalgia. Wonderful images, all carefully captioned with informative and witty text, will help reader's return to the last century without ever leaving the armchairs in which they sit. As you turn each leaf you will be able to share those days when dad was a lad or grandma was a flapper. Our towns and boroughs have changed so much since their times that it is hard to bring to mind just how everything used to be. Thank goodness for the camera. Without a pictorial record so much of our recent history would be a mere memory. You know how unreliable memories are because the mind can play tricks, but the camera never lies. All the pictures and photographs are accompanied by words that sharpen the recollections you might have. Some readers will have personal experience of the scenes laid out within, while other images will bring back to mind the stories that parents and grandparents told. In this book you will be able to see what it was they were talking about when referring to certain streets and events. There are other photographs and memory joggers that you will be able to remember for yourself. Perhaps this book might even settle a wager or two. Quite often people remember the same occasion or place in different ways. If there is a fact or picture in this book that helps you win the bet, then good luck. However if it was your memory that was playing tricks, then you can always turn to the next page! There will be plenty more of interest to follow.

'More Manchester Memories is not intended to be a dry and dusty old history book. It is meant to be a means for the reader to indulge in a wave of nostalgia for a century that is not too far behind us, but is growing more distant with each passing day. The 20th century brought us so much. The aeroplane flew for the first time. Electrical appliances changed the way we ran our households and

entertained ourselves. Women were liberated and the country became a multicultural society. Villages grew into towns and industry replaced agriculture as our setting. New and ever wider roads swept away the lanes and cottages of our heritage. Little shops became supermarkets and tower blocks rose on the skyline.

The computer chip replaced the brain. Without pictorial records of the past we would only be able to rely on the written or spoken word for our nostalgia. But, with this latest in the series of True North publications, there is a chance to claw back those days of yesteryear. Sit your children down and leaf through the book with them. They are our future, but they must not be allowed to ignore their heritage. Make sure that they have cameras of their own so that they can repeat the process for generations to come. They must learn from our mistakes and build on our successes. Nostalgia does not mean that you are wallowing in the past. You are just remembering the good times and shedding a silent tear for when it was less than so. Not everything in your background is wonderful, but it would be a crime to fail to preserve those bits that were.

Manchester is a vibrant and ever evolving city and, as all true Mancunians will tell you, is the capital of the north. Any scousers from Liverpool or loiners from Leeds can argue about which of their cities comes next. However, it must be admitted that our home was once little more than a humble backwater.

There was little life to be seen in AD 79 when the Romans built a fort on the Irwell, in the vicinity of the present Castlefield, that they called Mancunium or Mamuciam, meaning 'breast shaped hill'. A small settlement developed beyond the walls that increased in size after the invaders departed and various Angles, Saxons and Danes took it in turns to be the dominant tribe. When it was the Normans' turn to dominate, further habitation took place around the church that was eventually to metamorphose into Manchester Cathedral. 'Mameceaster', as it became known during this period, was recognised as a free market town in 1301 when Thomas de Gresley granted it a charter. The Market Place, between Cateaton Street and St Mary's Gate, began to prosper. Even so, growth was still only gradual. There was evidence of a woollen textile cottage industry, but the great days still lay ahead.

The town was not without its troubles, particularly during the English Civil War. It took the side of the Parliamentarians against Charles I and found itself besieged by 4,000 Royalists in 1642. Showing steadfast resolve, Manchester held out and the king's troops moved off and plundered Bolton

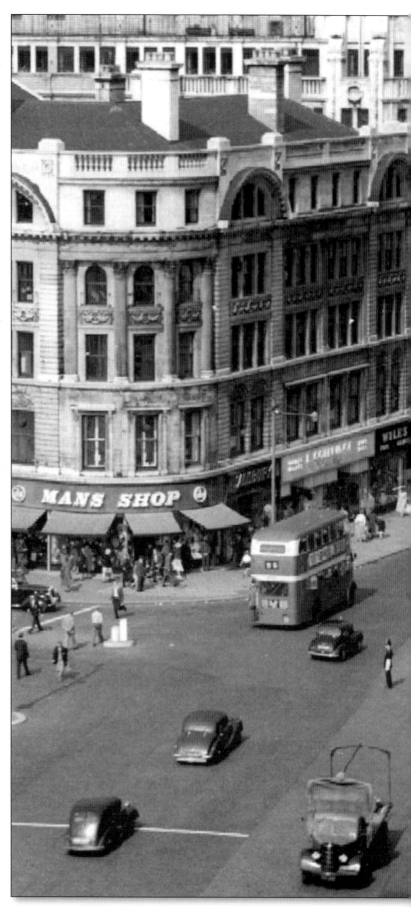

instead! Just over a century later, the military arrived again. On this occasion the forces belonged to Bonnie Prince Charlie, and residents were forced to support the Young Pretender's cause. By now, Manchester was beginning to start on its road to fame and fortune. The population in the middle of the 18th century was still only in the region of just over 15,000, but a different sort of monarch was on his way. This would be the time when King Cotton ushered in the boom years and our city took on its nickname of 'Cottonopolis'. Improvements in spinning, notably by Hargreaves at Blackburn in 1767 and other pioneers such as Arkwright, enabled Manchester's textile output to increase and by 1789 the town's population had grown to almost 50,000. By this time the age of steam was firmly entered and in 1789 a steam engine was built in Manchester for the manufacture of cotton and power looms were introduced the following year. This enabled cotton output to be increased to levels as yet unknown. The industrial revolution was well and truly off and running.

Allied to the introduction of mechanisation in its textile industry, Manchester benefited from other developments. In 1721 improvements were made to the Rivers Irwell and Mersey with the enforcement of the Mersey Irwell Navigation Act. Much larger vessels could now reach Manchester and ensured its development as an 'inland port'. Road improvements were also being made and in 1724 the first turnpike road in the area was opened providing a link with the spa town of Buxton in Derbyshire. Between 1759 and 1761 James Brindley constructed the Bridgewater Canal at the authorisation of the Bridgewater Canal Act. It was the first modern artificial waterway and it linked Manchester to coal mines at Worsley to the North West. This provided a regular and efficient supply of coal, necessary for an industrialised town. The age of steam also brought the railways and from 1826 to 1830 the Liverpool and Manchester Railway was built. By this time there were over 100 spinning factories in the town and the population soared to around 180,000 at the start of the 19th century and rocketed to 500,000 by its end. Manchester was in its prime.

Now that our stroll down memory lane has reached the 20th century, put an old 78 on the record player and listen to Henry Hall's band as you chew a licorice stick and sup a glass of Chester's dark mild reminiscing about tanners and farthings and the days when children were kids and not mini adults. Enjoy the nostalgia rush of 'More Manchester Memories'.

AT LEISURE

Tell the grandchildren to come and have a look at this photograph. They might think that 'Strictly Come Dancing' was a special 21st century television programme that invented the form of entertainment called ballroom dancing. Of course we all know that it was one of the most popular pastimes during the first half of the last century, and not just indoors either as we can see from this prewar scene at Belle Vue. The wooden, open air platform resounded to the sound of dancing feet as couples strutted their stuff with spin turns, fishtail steps and a neatly executed chassé or two in the quickstep, waltz or foxtrot. Nearly everybody knew how to perform these dances and could also

throw in a few Latin American ones, such as the cha-cha, rumba and samba. They were necessary social skills that many children learned at Saturday classes and put into practice at church hops or more formal occasions. The jumping around and wild gyrations observed in the modern club scene has no comparison with the style and grace displayed on a proper dance floor. Every town had its own ballroom, some more than one. Resident bands played live music and some of them went on to fame and fortune playing on the radio, in summer seasons and cutting records. The Joe Loss Band was still having chart success in the 1960s with 'Must be Madison' and 'March of the Mods'.

Below: Rowing boats were for hire on the lake in Belle Vue and many took the opportunity to flex their muscles and pretend that they were competitors in the annual University Boat Race. Others let someone else do the work and availed themselves of a ride on the 'Little Eastern' paddle steamer. Ironically named after Brunel's mighty ocean going liner 'Great Eastern', the Belle Vue version gave families the chance to relax and take in the view across the grounds on their journey around the lake. In 1858 John Jennison leased a triangular area of land at the junction of Hyde Road and Kirkmanshulme Lane and created the Great Lake. The first lake was circular but in 1876 it was enlarged and made into more of a pear shape. The Lake Hotel opened in July of that same year and the Lake Entrance was created. These took advantage of the opening of the nearby Belle Vue Railway Station. The 1878 guide to the zoological gardens states that 'this is

the most convenient entrance for people arriving from the Midland Railway' and that 'commodious stables

have been erected in connection with the hotel at this entrance'. Just to give a flavour of the different classes of visitor at the time, the guide goes on to say that 'the admission to the gardens for coachmen and servants accompanying each carriage is the same as for any other visitor'.

Left: During the last war Piccadilly Gardens lost its flower beds and lawns when they were dug up during the Dig for Victory campaign. This slogan became one of the most memorable of those used during the 1939-45 war. The whole of Britain was encouraged to transform their own gardens into small allotments to combat the shortage of food. It was hoped that this would not only provide much needed vegetables for families and neighbourhoods, but also help the war effort by freeing up valuable space for war materials on the merchant ships. In just over just a few months Britain was

transformed, with gardens, flowerbeds and parks dug up for the planting of vegetables. The propaganda campaign the Ministry of Food had put in place was a success and it was estimated that over 1,400,000 people had allotments. By 1943, over a million tons of vegetables were being grown in both gardens and allotments. As soon as possible, once peace was

declared, Piccadilly Gardens returned to normality and the flowers bloomed again, giving Mancunian workers a delightful spot where they good while away a few spare minutes at lunchtime. The air raid shelters on the far side of the ornamental gardens were used by those caught in the city centre who did not have time to get home or to another place of safety when the sirens sounded.

Below: The ABC Cinema on Deansgate was still well patronised when 'A Kind of Loving' was the main attraction in 1962. Based on a Stan Barstow novel, the script was written by Keith Waterhouse and Willis Hall. Starring the darkly handsome Alan Bates and the lovely June Ritchie, it was one of a genre of kitchen sink and gritty dramas popular in the late 1950s and early 1960s. Alan Bates (1934-2003) had made his name on the West End stage in the 1956 production of John Osborne's 'Look Back in Anger'. He had a long and illustrious career on stage and in film and was knighted a few months before his untimely death. June Ritchie, just 23 when this film was made, had much less impact in her career than her co-star. She continued to work spasmodically, relying on occasional television work to keep her name in lights. The ABC was part of a cinema chain that merged with the Odeon group earlier this century, but by then it had been turned into a pub. Cinema going was at its most popular either side of the last war, but television and bingo struck a double whammy and audiences dwindled. It is only in the last few years, with the coming of multiplexes, that the tills in box offices have started to ring merrily once more.

Firework Island on the lake in Belle Vue was the hub of all celebrations held there every November 5th. For many years either side of the second world war this was the place to be to witness huge displays of pyrotechnics as gigantic Catherine wheels whirled, figures on metal frameworks burst into colourful life as sparks showered the night sky and mammoth rockets thundered into the sky drawing oohs and aahs from the massed multitude below. The island was not limited to firework displays, nor did it just function on one day each year. There were battle enactments as great events in British and world history were recreated, often including lots of bangs and crashes to use up the leftover gunpowder from the previous Bonfire Night. There were also more sedate and cultural performances, with ballet and drama being performed on the island. We do not know what the attraction was on this day in 1949, but the vast majority look to have been enthralled with whatever the production was. In the mid 1950s the firework displays were toned down and, naturally, the public's taste for something more sophisticated took them towards more dramatic entertainment. Audiences dwindled and the last rip was rapped in 1969.

Above: All the fun of the fair was to be had at Belle Vue. The large entertainment complex had so much to offer the general public that the variety on offer provided interest for folk of all ages and from every walk of life. In the fairground there were the traditional rides, some of which might seem tame to today's youth. However, we enjoyed the dodgems, the waltzers, the tunnel of love and the Ocean Wave. In other parts of the grounds we could experience the animals in the zoo or watch Jackie Pye, Bert Royal, Masambula and the Simba Kid grunt and groan in grappling contests at the King's Hall. Speedway and greyhound racing fans were well catered for and Belle Vue was truly Manchester's main centre of entertainment. It was founded in 1836 by John Jennison (1793-1869) on a site between Hyde Road and Kirkmanshulme Lane. It was the third oldest zoological garden in the United Kingdom and the country's most important provincial zoo. In 1847 the first guide book was published, a maze was added to the gardens and a racecourse built near the Longsight entrance. The Jennison family sold the enterprise to Belle Vue (Manchester) Ltd in 1925. By then, the zoo, King's Hall and a funfair were all well established.

Below: In 1950 cyclists participated in one of several 50 mile races held at Heaton Park each year. This has always been one of the most popular sports for Mancunians and the Bury athlete, Reg Harris (1929-92), was the main local cyclist to come to national prominence around this time. He won two silver medals in the 1948 London Olympics before becoming the World Amateur Sprint Champion in 1949, 1950, 1951, 1952 and 1954. He died in Macclesfield in June 1992 after collapsing while still riding his bike at the age of 72! A memorial statue to his memory stands in the Manchester Velodrome. His name was often used when accosting speeding bike riders with the rhetorical question, 'Who do you think you are, Reg Harris?' The young man, hand on hip gazing across the parkland, sported a quif hairstyle that was to be popular for most of the decade. Held in place with a liberal application of Brylcreem, it was his fashion statement in an era before the phrase had been invented. Heaton Park is the largest municipal park in Europe. The former estate of the Earls of Wilton has been owned by Manchester City Council since 1902 and represents an amazing 25 per cent of the green space in Manchester. About one million people crowded through its gates in 1982 to hear Pope John-Paul II say Mass.

Above: In 1958 the Gaumont, Chorlton-cum-Hardy, was showing a double feature. 'The Whole Truth', a black and white British movie, told the story of a jealous husband who murders his wife and tries to frame another for the crime. It starred the famous names of Stewart Granger, George Raft and Donna Reed. The 'B' movie, 'Return to Warbow', based on one of Les Savage's Wild West books, had Phil Carey in the leading role. Carey's main claim to fame was his supporting role in the popular Doris Day-Howard Keel musical, 'Calamity Jane'. However, the audience going through the doors in this photograph had no interest in these matters. This was Saturday and it was matinee time for the children. They were turned loose in their dozens by parents happy to get a couple of hours peace and quiet. Inside the auditorium the kiddies hooted with joy at the antics of the Three Stooges and thrilled to the adventures of Flash Gordon as he found himself hopelessly entrapped by the evil machinations of Ming the Merciless. Quite how he could manage to escape seemed an impossibility, but escape he did, week after week in this popular serial. Slightly older boys were hooked on the actresses playing Dale Arden and Princess Aura, while prepubescent girls took a shine to Larry 'Buster' Crabbe in the role of the hero.

The All England School Athletic Championships were held at Belle Vue Stadium in 1955. During this decade, crowds were large at any sporting event. Soccer stadiums were full, queues formed outside Old Trafford cricket ground for county cricket matches that nowadays play to just a handful, athletics had a large following and speedway packed them in. Even such events as wrestling promotions, laced with a high degree of 'codology', posted 'house full' notices. We do not know if any of the competitors in this photograph went on to achieve international recognition, but they had a number of role models to give them encouragement. Roger Bannister ran the first sub four minute mile in 1954 and middle distance runner Chris Chataway thrilled crowds when he beat the much vaunted Russian Vladimir Kuts. Gordon Pirie added numbers to the crowd when it was learned that he was to run at the White City, near Old Trafford, and Yorkshire's Derek Ibbotson would set a new record for the mile in 1957. Olympic medallists Shirley Cawley, Sheila Lerwill and Thelma Hopkins provided female inspiration and Diane Leather shocked the world when she became the first woman to run a sub five minute mile three weeks after Bannister's race. The central field at the stadium was formerly used by the professional rugby league side, Belle Vue Rangers.

Above: Soccer is the beautiful game, but it was very much the province of the ordinary man in the street before the likes of Sky TV, Russian billionaires and the advertising brigade got their hands on it. Games used to kick off at 3 pm on a Saturday and, apart from the occasional Wednesday night FA Cup replay, that was that. Fans travelling to a match early enough to get a good spot on the terraces might well share a seat on the bus with one of the players they were going to cheer on that same afternoon. Manchester United's Old Trafford has seen major remodelling over the years since this September 1959 photograph was taken. Like everywhere else, in the wake of the Hillsborough disaster it has become all seater and the sight of swaying masses on the Stretford End is no more. But, the ground is still packed for every home game, just as it was nearly half a century ago. Then, the club was recovering from the bitter blow of the Munich air disaster that had killed half of the first team squad in February 1958 when United was on its way back home from a victory over Red Star Belgrade in the European Cup quarter final. Hopeful fans thronged into the ground during 1959-60, but it was to be one of several mediocre seasons for the Reds.

Right: As children we loved to take donkey rides on the sands at Blackpool or Rhyl, but Belle Vue offered something more dramatic. With shades of the Raj and Kipling, an elephant ride had something much more exotic to offer. The patient pachyderm tolerated the kiddies who clambered on board and off she went in a lumbering gait as happy souls called out to their watching parents. Children took the scenic railway ride, watched the chimps having their tea and then joined the jungle express, swaying in their perches as the great beast ambled around the gardens. There were always long queues by the platform from which the riders got on board, but as about a dozen took the ride at any one go the waiting time was acceptable and well worth it. No doubt do-gooders today would think it was cruel to the animals, but they seemed well cared for and even tempered.

EVENTS OF THE 1950s

WHAT'S ON?

Television hit Britain in a big way during the 1950s. Older readers will surely remember 'Double Your Money, Dixon of Dock Green and 'Dragnet' (whose characters' names were changed 'to protect the innocent'). Commercial television was introduced on 22nd September 1955, and Gibbs SR toothpaste were drawn out of the hat to become the first advert to be shown. Many believed adverts to be vulgar, however, and audiences were far less than had been hoped for.

GETTING AROUND

The year 1959 saw the development of the world's first practical air-cushion vehicle - better known to us as the hovercraft. The earliest model was only able to travel at slow speeds over very calm water and was unable to carry more than three passengers. The faster and smoother alternative to the sea ferry quickly caught on, and by the 1970s a 170-ton car-carrying hovercraft service had been introduced across the English Channel.

SPORTING CHANCE

The four-minute mile had remained the record since 1945, and had become regarded as virtually unbreakable. On 6th May 1954, however, Oxford University student Roger Bannister literally ran away with the record, accomplishing the seemingly impossible in three minutes 59.4 seconds. Bannister collapsed at the end of his last amazing lap, even temporarily losing his vision. By the end of the day, however, he had recovered sufficiently to celebrate his achievement in a London night club!

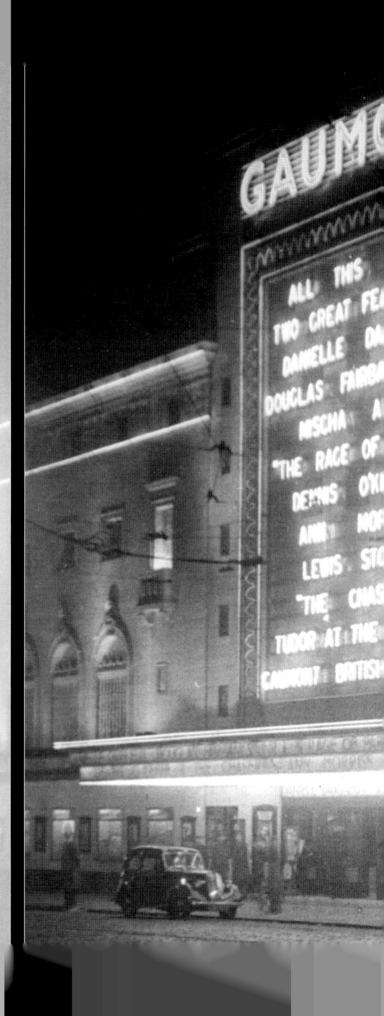

Glowing like a beacon in the night sky, Chorlton-cum-Hardy's Gaumont Cinema was later to become the ABC. It underwent several name changes during its lifetime. It originally opened as the Picture Palace in 1922, but changed name to the Savoy in 1928. It was one of the first cinemas in suburban Manchester that could show the new talking pictures. That transition marked a significant move in the careers of many movie actors. Some handsome leading men who had made women swoon in the aisles with their sultry looks had voices that ranged form the squeaky to the incoherent and their names swiftly disappeared from the billboards. Others, such as Douglas Fairbanks, made a seamless move from one form of cinema to the other. The Gaumont boasted a mighty Wurlitzer organ on which audiences were entertained before the main show began. It has the distinction of being where the musical Gibb Brothers first appeared on stage. The trio began singing when Maurice and his twin Robin were six and elder brother Barry was nine. They had been going to mime to a record at the cinema, but the record was broken en route and the brothers had to perform live instead. A few years later they emigrated to Australia and went on the find fame and fortune as the Bee Gees. They returned to Chorlton in 1996 while filming a documentary about their childhood. Barry subsequently bought the old family home in Keppel Road. After its closure in 1966 the cinema became a funeral parlour.

Above: Nellie the elephant packed her trunk and set off with her pals into town to advertise the circus at Belle Vue. A long train of animals, jugglers, acrobats and men on stilts accompanied the floats that promoted the show. The internationally acclaimed circus was perhaps the most popular draw to Belle Vue and every year acts would perform from all over Europe in the 'big top' (Kings Hall). As it became less politically correct to have animal acts in the show the circus struggled to survive and eventually closed in 1982. A circus was introduced to Belle Vue in the late 1920s with former Blackpool Tower ringmaster George Lockhart in charge. In this photograph we can see part of the Billy Smart name on one of the trucks in front of the trolleybus. It was in 1946 that the first ever Billy Smart's Circus appeared at Southall Park and then toured alongside Smart's Funfair. It became incredibly successful with the postwar general public and featured regularly on early BBC television programmes. Televised Christmas and Easter circus extravaganzas followed and made this one of the most famous of all this country's travelling circuses. At the height of its powers Billy Smart's Circus toured the whole of Britain with a huge 6,000 seater big top, an army of international circus artistes and a 200 strong host of elephants, lions, horses, polar bears, camels, sealions and chimpanzees.

Below: Many of the facilities at Belle Vue were closed during World War II, so it was no surprise to see thousands queuing to gain admission in 1946 once the complex was fully functional again. Buses, trams, coaches, the railway and private cars poured their passengers in through the entrances to the pleasure grounds that had been entertaining visitors for over a century. Until its closure in the 1970s, and the subsequent sale and redevelopment of the site, Belle Vue attracted millions of happy, satisfied customers. Although fashions change and people develop wider interests as the years roll by, it seemed that Belle Vue had enough variety to help it go on forever. However, things were not helped when fire struck the grounds in 1958. On 17 January the ballroom was devastated in a major blaze that gutted the art studio and destroyed thousands of musical scores. The whole block that included a ballroom, cafes, shops, bars and the firework viewing stand were lost. The total cost of the damage was estimated to be in the region of £250,000. The outdoor dance floor, which was at one time used as a roller skating surface, also fell victim to the flames. Another fire in 1964 destroyed the Cumberland and Windermere suites, as well as damaging the speedway stadium. Major repair work after these incidents disrupted many activities and the public found new outlets to satisfy their leisure needs.

STREET SCENES

The view from Portland Street across Piccadilly in 1936 illustrates what a peaceful and pleasant area this once was. There is no Piccadilly Plaza or high rise office and hotel blocks. The gardens are just as the city fathers intended, gentle and tranquil and just the place to relax while the commerce of the city carries on around them. People strolling along the paths or sitting on the benches enjoyed the serenity of the spot.

The domed building at the top centre now belongs to Debenham's. It was originally built after the first world war as a cotton warehouse for the Rylands family. John Rylands (1801-88) was a well-to-do local manufacturer and merchant. His commercial abilities and eye for an opportunity were to make him one of the wealthiest men in Manchester. The 19th century was a boom time for 'king cotton' and Rylands was the leading player in textiles in Great Britain. His father had worked in the same industry, so the young Rylands had a good grounding in the family business of Rylands and Sons, in Wigan. He brought the business to Manchester in 1823 when he opened a warehouse at 11 New High Street.

As with many prosperous Victorians, he cared about the lot of his fellows and made substantial do nations to establish orphanages, libraries and homes for the aged.

Below: The day had dawned dark and grey over Piccadilly on this day in 1936. People milled about in the gardens and on the esplanade and some even wished one another 'Good morning'. Heaven help anyone who did that today. He would be greeted with the sort of look that suggested he was out of his mind or even be accused of harassment. Those with mobile phones clamped to their ears would not even notice. Those with something to say to their companions strolling along the road would have commented on the state of the nation and that across Europe. They were difficult times for everyone. In March, the stomp of the jackboot sounded in the cities of the Rhineland as Hitler's army reoccupied its backyard in defiance of the Treaty of Versailles. Mussolini's forces forced Abyssinia (Ethiopia) to surrender to Italian rule and civil war broke out in Spain. The Fascists were flexing their military muscles and the first stormclouds of war began to gather over Europe. At home, we had our own major constitutional crisis when King Edward VIII decided to abandon the British throne and go into exile with his future bride, the already twice divorced American socialite, Wallis Simpson. Many members of the working classes could not have cared less as they had enough to worry about trying to make ends meet. In October, 200 unemployed men set off from Jarrow to march to London in an attempt to heighten awareness of their plight.

Above: The drivers were waiting to turn into the car park at Old Trafford, the home of Lancashire County Cricket Club, in 1959. Test matches still attract large crowds today, but back then three day county cricket pulled in large numbers, especially if the opposition was Yorkshire or the mighty Surrey. Lancashire had a strong side in the 1950s. Openers Winston Place and Cyril Washbrook provided a good platform for the likes of all rounder Alan Wharton and spinners Bob Berry and Roy Tattersall. When a young Brian Statham was unleashed on the opposition his speed and accuracy helped secure many a victory. Later in the decade, batsman Geoff Pullar was a constant thorn in the sides of other teams and there were a number who could not fathom the legspin of the unorthodox Tommy Greenhough. When one-day cricket came along in the 1960s, Lancashire ruled the roost under the leadership of Jackie Bond. Many of the players were local lads, brought up via an apprenticeship in the schools of hard knocks known as the Lancashire League and Central Lancashire League.

Below: It seems that every few years someone has a go at digging up parts of Piccadilly. The usual mess of lorries, concrete mixers, piping and debris accompanied this latest assault on the area in 1957. An interesting, but ironic, comment can be made on observing the airline advert on the building on the far side of Piccadilly. It was being recommended that we 'Fly BEA Viscount'. Half a century ago, the foreign holiday industry was still in its

Above: The Alhambra Theatre opened in 1910 and was immediately popular as a music hall. The upper circle was known to locals as 'the gods' and, after its rear was converted to a cinema known as the Pavilion, the building continued in this dual purpose role until 1916 when the theatre audiences declined to the extent that this section closed. However, somewhat confusingly, the cinema was transferred to the Alhambra part and the Pavilion was given over to dancing! Naughty children used to patronise 'the gods' and shower people below with lolly sticks and empty ice cream tubs as they dodged the torch beams of the usherettes attempting to locate the culprits. The Alhambra, situated on Ashton Old Road, Openshaw at the junction with Ogden Lane, was also used as a boxing venue during the interwar years. The dance hall became known as Chick Hibberts and was notorious as it seemed that there was always a rumble as the dance turned out and the immediate area was regularly patrolled by police expecting trouble. The main battles came in the era of the Teddy Boys in the 1950s and responsible parents banned their teenagers from frequenting the place. The Alhambra closed its doors in 1960, a victim of the changing trends in entertainment that closed many similar businesses.

infancy. A week at Butlin's was more to the taste and pocket of the man in the street. Even going to Anglesey was akin to travelling abroad. Some middle class families dipped their toes in foreign waters, but even these were in the minority. But, we gradually began to take the plunge and package holidays across the Channel or even as far afield as sunny Spain, were tried for the first time. British European Airways (BEA) promoted such exploratory zeal.

However, many people were nervous of taking to the air for the first time and setbacks such as occurred on 17 March 1957 did little to allay their fears. BEA announced the grounding of its turbo-prop Viscounts when one crashed at Ringway Airport, killing 22. The company would suffer another terrible loss less than a year later when the Ambassador aircraft carrying the Busby Babes crashed at Munich.

Above: In 1946 the noble horse was still to be found as part of the transport system in urban areas. In back streets rag and bone men came round in their carts, chimney sweeps came with their tackle and window cleaners arrived bearing their ladders, buckets and 'shammy' leathers. Gardeners eagerly awaited their appearance as they prepared to sweep up behind them, searching out additives for their rhubarb and roses. Even the town and city centres still heard the sound of clip-clopping hooves and here we can see an example of a magnificent beast somewhat dangerously cutting in between a Pilcher tram and the bus to Monton. To the right, a handsome Rolls Royce acts as a fiscal contrast to horse and cart. The owners are obviously from opposite ends of the social spectrum. Victoria Station approach is to the left and we can just make out the period railings marking the entrance to subterranean toilets. Manchester Cathedral dominates this part of Victoria Street. Built in a perpendicular, Gothic style, the cathedral marks the centre of medieval Manchester. It was dedicated by Henry V to St Mary, St Denys and St George. Much of the exterior of the building is a 19th century reconstruction carried out by Joseph Crowther who was faithful to the original building in his designs so that none of the original styling has been lost.

Below: The Gaiety Theatre used to occupy the spot where ABC Weekend Television stood in 1965. The building is a typical example of the sort of architecture that planners dumped on our cities in the 1960s. They appeared to be incapable of thinking in other than straight lines and so all their ideas were turned into squares and oblongs of uniformity. Such structures were without soul or character and could have been created by a four year old with a ruler. Contrast it with the imaginative Central Library, full of curves, grace and intricacy. There really is no comparison in class. The Associated British Corporation (ABC) was one of a number of commercial television companies set up in the 1950s by cinema chains in an attempt to safeguard their business by getting involved in television which was taking away their cinema audiences. It began transmitting from the midlands in February 1956 before opening a studio in Didsbury the following May. The first programme from this studio was coverage of Manchester City's defeat of Birmingham City in the FA Cup Final, famous for goalie Bert Trautmann's broken neck. A string of popular programmes, such as 'Armchair Theatre', 'The Avengers' and 'Opportunity Knocks' gave ABC a fine reputation, though comedian Bob Monkhouse thought little of it, referring to the initials as meaning 'All B***** Commercials'! The company ceased operating in 1968 and evolved with others into Thames Television.

As the 1950s drew to a close, the future for traditional cinema was looking bleak. Television had made major inroads into movie audiences, particularly among the older generation who preferred the comfort of its own fireside to making a journey in all weathers to a building that might be just a little bit draughty. Bingo also made its move into the arena. This was something different and could not be covered by television, so many cinemas started to make the transition into bingo halls. The Regal on Oxford Road opened as a brand spanking new building in 1930 that contained two cinemas with a combined seating total of 1,600. Not surprisingly, there were known as the Regal Twins and, as purpose-built cinemas, offered the very latest state of the art technology in very comfortable surroundings. Some other picture houses were converted theatres or musical halls and lacked many of the modern features of purpose built cinemas. Partly because of its more up to date style, the Regal weathered the storm of television and saw off the challenge of the call of 'legs eleven'. In 1972 it was converted into a five screen enterprise, but closed down in 1986. Over the intervening years since this photograph was taken, Oxford Road has become busier and busier, often clogged with traffic coming from the direction of Fallowfield and Withington along Wilmslow Road.

Left: Manchester achieved city status in 1853. Exactly a century later, it celebrated the coronation of Queen Elizabeth II. Albert Square was decorated with streamers, bunting and Union flags as we shared the nation's joy in seeing a new and young monarch at the helm. Perhaps she would be able to assist in the ushering in of a new Elizabethan age; one that would help drive out the last vestiges of austerity that still lingered on eight years after the war. She would grow in maturity during the second half of the century as our own fortunes improved, or such was the hope. The occasion was one that would unite the country again in similar way to the parties that took place to celebrate VE and VJ Day in 1945. The Labour government had tried to promote national unity with the 1951 Festival of Britain, but that event provoked as much grumbling about cost as it did enjoyment. However, there was something different about a royal occasion. We could all share. It was also one of the first public events to have national television coverage. Although only a minority owned receivers, most people knew someone in their neighbourhood who possessed a set. On that damp morning in June 1953, certain householders suddenly became very popular as dozens crowded into their front rooms to watch the events at Westminster Abbey unfurl on a black and white, flickering screen in the corner of the room.

Above: On 2 June 1953, the young woman who was to become one of the longest reigning monarchs this country has ever had was crowned by the Archbishop of Canterbury, Dr Fisher. Manchester's Albert Square was decorated in honour of the occasion and the Union flag flew proudly on the Town Hall. The square was named for Queen Victoria's consort, her much loved husband who died young in 1861, aged just 42. On his death from typhoid fever, the British public, which had regarded him almost as an enemy alien, finally recognised his exceptional qualities. Throughout almost 40 years of widowhood the Queen decided important questions on the basis of what she thought Albert would have done. The square has now been largely pedestrianised and regularly serves as a venue for local events, celebrations and street fairs. Over half a century ago, traffic flowed either side of the toilets and the Albert Memorial. Acting as the entrance to Manchester Town Hall, Albert Square pays tribute to one of Greater Manchester's architects. There is a series of monumental statues, including the Albert Memorial that was an earlier and smaller inspiration for the London one. Constructed by the Manchester architect Thomas Worthington, it dates from 1862-67 and the figure of Albert is by Mathew Noble. All the statues in the square face towards the Town Hall. These include Oliver Heywood by Theed, Gladstone by Raggi and a stone John Bright by A. Bruce Joy.

Above: Manchester Garages on Oxford Road was, in 1970, the city's principal Ford dealer. This was the start of the decade when laws would be passed in Britain determining equal pay for women and the Methodist Church would open its doors to female ministers. Later in the 70s Britain would have a woman in charge at 10 Downing Street for the only time. Things were changing, albeit gradually. Life was to become interesting for car dealerships as well. The trickle of vehicles from the Far East became a cascade as Datsun, Toyota and Honda were at the vanguard of a wave of imports that rocked the status quo. Where BMC and Ford had dominated, their stranglehold on the business was loosened dramatically. Although Ford was an American name, the company's British manufacturing arm was important to the company. It was also a major employer that played a strong role in the home economy. Over the years such places as Trafford Park, Dagenham, Halewood, Swansea and Daventry had employed thousands of people whose livelihood depended on the success of the company. As the yen began to rival the dollar, angry workers made their voices known. The 1970s would become a troubled decade for industrial unrest when miners and power workers added their weight to the union cause. Three day weeks and a winter of discontent were on the way.

The girders belong to the Mancunian Way, the inner city ring road that was supposed to solve congestion problems on the city roads. Like all such schemes, it helped but failed to provide a solution. Highway planners really do need to think more radically about coming up with plans that will completely change the nature of our roads and motoring habits, rather than just tinker with the status quo by adding an odd carriageway here or a spur road there. Dubbed 'the highway in the sky', it was completed in 1967, with an extended section added 25 years later. The Mancunian Way forms the southern section of the ironically titled 'Manchester and Salford Inner Relief Route'. The A57 from Liverpool in the west to Lincoln in the east runs along this highway as far as the A6 junction where it becomes the A635 through east Manchester, Tameside and across the Pennines to Doncaster. Its name was chosen by schoolchildren who entered a competition to select an appropriate title. Once opened, the Mancunian Way fulfilled its basic purpose, providing a vital east-west artery and saving the city centre from total gridlock. But the growth in traffic had been woefully underestimated by road planners, and soon the queues lengthened, especially at the approaches to the roundabouts at either end. It is also an ugly concrete blight and the intended pedestrian areas within its roundabouts have become dangerous, no go areas.

Left: Corporation Street was completed in 1851 as a relief road for the heavy traffic on Market Street, one of the main arterial routes out of Manchester in early Victorian times. Many of the buildings that were built around that time were demolished shortly after this 1958 photograph was taken, making way for the next generation of retail outlets, offices and pubs. Further transformations would include Marks and Spencer and the Arndale Centre in this vicinity. The street came to national notice on Saturday 15 June 1996 when the IRA placed a bomb in a Ford van and detonated some 1,500 kg of high explosive. It was the largest such device seen in Britain and, although no-one was killed as warnings had been given, over 200 people still suffered some form of injury from the blast that was heard up to 10 miles away. Several buildings close to the centre of the explosion had to be demolished and many more were closed for months afterwards to allow structural repairs. Nearly half a century ago, times were less troubled. The country had begun to turn the corner after the near decade of postwar austerity it had suffered as it struggled to get back on its economic feet. By now we had reached the Macmillan 'never had it so good' phase as unemployment was low, rationing a thing of the past and a feel-good factor filled the air.

Below: Mancunians will tell you that the music hall joke about the city being famous for its damp climate is based on a myth. Unfortunately, when presented with evidence like this it is hard to mount a defence. This day in 1958 was gloomy, wet and fairly miserable. The pavements on King Street glistened with water that had dropped from the skies during a constant drizzle throughout the day, making the surroundings appear lacklustre. It also dampened the spirits of shoppers who were only too happy to call it a day and head off home. There was little opportunity for the owner of the soft top coupe parked at the kerbside to enjoy the exhilaration of bowling along the road with the wind whistling through his hair. On a better day you could just imagine a young man, sporting a pair of leather-backed driving gloves, showing off to everybody in the way that Lonnie Donegan described in his hit record 'Putting on the style'. But, today was not the one for lowering the hood. Sadly, it has to be admitted, the 1950s sometimes saw notices posted at Old Trafford cricket ground saying, 'Match abandoned without a ball being bowled'. Such examples of our northern weather gave more ammunition to the southern softies who liked to jest at our expense.

Sykes Seafoods - Hooked by fish

It's a little known fact that most fish and chip shop cooking ranges are made in Halifax in West Yorkshire. Most of them have labels on them saying who manufactured them. The fish that go into the ranges to be cooked however are anonymous. Though if they did have labels it's a good bet that a very great many of them indeed had passed through Manchester and the firm of Sykes Seafoods.

Manchester's New Smithfield Market in Whitworth Street East, Openshaw opened it doors for business in 1973. The old Manchester Smithfield Market which the new building, on a 30 acre site, replaced had been opened in 1853 some 120 years earlier: at its peak at the turn of the last century, this site was probably the largest market complex in Britain, occupying seven acres. In 1987 the site was designated a conservation area and has since been sympathetically regenerated as part of a £7.5m residential and leisure development.

The Wet Fish Market is open Monday - Saturday for customers to come in and buy fresh and frozen fish. Best

known amongst the many firms operating from the new market is J Sykes & Sons Ltd, seafood wholesalers and distributors. The business was first incorporated as a limited company in 1948. Today the holding company Sykes Seafoods Ltd, established in 1996, has three trading subsidiaries: J Sykes & Sons (Manchester) Ltd, created in 1948, J Sykes & Sons (Fish merchants) Ltd, formed in 1996 and J Sykes & Sons (North West) Ltd, which began as recently as 2005.

But though the firm may have only had a history as a limited company for six decades its story and that of the Sykes family goes back almost as far as that of the old market.

Today J. Sykes & Sons Ltd imports seafood from all over the world for onward distribution throughout the United Kingdom. The company supplies Food Service, Wholesale, Retail, Catering and Fish Frying businesses from its product range of over 500 lines. Respected seafood brands which the business offers include Arctic Royal, Royal Greenland, Young's Seafoods, Paramount 21, Whitby Seafoods and Bantry Bay Seafoods.

The business was originally started by Joseph Sykes, the great grandfather of the present owners Martin and David Sykes. Joe Sykes started trading wet fish and Dutch

Pictures: *At work inside old Smithfield Market.*

shrimps from the original Smithfield Market in 1862, in the heart of Manchester City Centre, with deliveries being made by horse and cart well into the 20th Century.

Though the availability of fresh fish and other seafood seems perfectly commonplace today their availability in Manchester in the 1860s was something which previous generations would have regarded as almost miraculous.

Until the middle of the Victorian era fresh seafood was available in quantity only at the seaside ports where the fish was actually landed. True some made it inland, but only at great expense: living fish would be transported in barrels by packhorse, the ultimate price reflecting the high cost of transport.

For the working classes sea-caught fish was still available, but unless one lived near the sea it would have been preserved by smoking or salting. Kippers not wet fish were the order of the day.

Ice and speed would provide the answer to the problems of supplying fresh fish to the growing city of Manchester.

The speed and relatively low cost of transport would be provided by Britain's ever-growing network of railways. The 31 mile length of the Liverpool & Manchester railway was opened on 15th September 1830 making it possible for

Above: *To the right can be seen the J Sykes & Sons premises in the old Smithfield Market.*

the first time for freshly caught fish to reach the hungry folk in Manchester within hours of landing. Other railway lines, and another technological development, would soon enable fresh fish to reach Manchester from much further away.

No matter how quickly fresh fish might be transported it was notoriously difficult to maintain that freshness, especially in warm weather. The answer to that problem was ice.

Ice had been used for centuries to preserve food and to cool drinks. Many large mansions boasted ice-houses, underground storage chambers where ice cut from lakes in winter could be stored for use in the summer months. In Victorian times this concept was extended to become for some decades a major commercial undertaking.

In the mid 19th century it was realised that the speed of steam ships and railways combined with the insulating properties of sawdust could make it economic to harvest vast quantities of ice from lakes in Canada and the around the Baltic and tranship it to warmer southern climes.

Now butchers, fishmongers, and even the better off home owner, could buy blocks of ice from an ice salesman which then could be kept for up to a week in zinc lined insulted boxes, the ancestor of the modern fridge – some of which were still in use as late as the 1950s.

Within a generation however, the transportation of lake ice over vast distances would be rendered unnecessary by the invention in 1876 of the commercially viable ice machine by Carl von Linde, a German engineer whose continuous process of liquefying gases in large quantities formed the basis for the modern technology of refrigeration– it would however, be many more decades before such exotic machines became cheap enough for individual businesses let alone individual homes to afford one of their own. For many years after the invention of the fridge the ice-man would still be making deliveries of ice to those fishmongers for whom ice was an essential part of their business.

Refrigeration not only made a difference to how long a fishmonger's stock would remain fresh, it also made a vast different to the supply of fish, and ultimately its price. Refrigerated trawlers would in due course mean than fishing vessels could travel further and return to port less frequently, increasing catch sizes and increasing profits whilst at the same time pushing down prices to the consumer. By the 1930s there was fish for everyone at a price they could afford. No wonder fish and chips became Britain's national dish and kept Britain fed through the Great Depression.

Following the second world war the business of J Sykes & Sons expanded greatly after the current owners' father Bill Sykes looked to the continent for supplies of fresh fish.

Ronald 'Bill' Sykes died in 1996, having worked in the firm until the previous year, by which time he was 75 years old having clocked up 60 years in the market trade. He had joined the family business in 1935 at the age of 15. At that time his father William and his uncles, Arthur and Charlie, were running the firm. By 1938, when Bill took over running the company at the extraordinarily young age of 18, it had become one of the largest wholesalers on the market.

For the next six decades Bill Sykes would be the driving force behind the business, taking it from local to national, and even international prominence.

The fact that there is still a viable fish market in Manchester is very largely due to Bill Sykes' efforts in the years immediately after the war when he provided the foundation for the future with his commercial courage in buying far more fish than he could ever sell and never refusing a good deal.

*Top: Bill Sykes, the driving force behind the business for six decades. **Above:** Present owners Martin Sykes (left) and David Sykes.*

During the 1950s a delivery service was started primarily delivering to fish fryers within a 10-mile radius of Manchester. Bill Sykes was soon moving 1,000 boxes of plaice and 1,000 of hake every week. The firm worked on a profit margin of two shillings (10p) per four stone box of Danish plaice in the 1960s, selling at around 30 shillings (£1.50) per stone. This particular part of the business would expand greatly in the 1990s mainly due to the increase in the quality of frozen-at-sea products. The variety of the frozen products which became available to the fish fryer would help keep them competitive against other takeaway foods, especially during periods when fresh fish prices have fluctuated greatly due to a shortage of supplies.

Chartered accountant Martin Sykes joined the business in 1965, his brother, fellow accountant David, joined five years later. By 1972 Sykes' was the biggest importer in England of Danish fish, particularly plaice, and later of cod and haddock fillets.

The company's big break had come in 1970 when Bill Sykes was asked to supply MacFisheries depots; Sykes' had been chosen because the firm was known throughout the trade for working for very small profit margins compared to its competitors. By the late 1970s MacFisheries had over 500 shops – and a large proportion of these was served by Sykes'.

The company relocated in 1974 to the new market 1.5 miles outside the city centre in order to take advantage of the growth in frozen seafood and has seen several expansions since, the most recent of which was the opening of a state-of-the art office and cold store building in 2005.

Expansion however has taken place despite serious setbacks. In the late 1970s the largest customer, MacFisheries, closed down and half of Sykes' business was gone. That event became the trigger for the company to begin to develop the catering side of the business.

The change in direction coincided with the move to the new market at Openshaw. In the old market the firm had no fewer than 17 stalls, but they were spread out in inconvenient locations. In moving to the new market Bill Sykes had ensured that all the Sykes' stalls were together.

Always thinking ahead Bill had also bought an acre of land adjacent to the fish market, a site which would in due course be the location of a 500-pallet cold store and offices from where the business would eventually be run.

J. Sykes & Sons imports seafood from all over the world for onward distribution: the Wholesale Division handles

An excellent distribution network, competitive pricing structure and extensive product range makes the firm the best choice for customers to use us as a one-stop-shop for all their seafood requirements rather than buying direct from manufacturers.

The Fish Fryers Division supplies cod, haddock and plaice in both fresh and frozen formats to fish and chip shops in Greater Manchester and throughout the North West.

full and mixed pallet orders for frozen fish and prawns all over the UK. The Fish Fryers Division supplies fish and chip shops in the North West of England with fresh & frozen fish, burgers, sausages, pies etc and full pallets of shatterpack cod & haddock nationally.

Recently the company has upgraded its own refrigerated transport fleet with new Volvo articulated lorries and Mercedes Benz Split-Temp vans, to ensure that customers' orders will arrive in the peak of condition - all very different from those early days when fish was delivered in open lorries, covered in ice.

Sykes' transports fish and shellfish all over England, Scotland, Wales and Ireland and supplements this service with additional back-up cover from outside hauliers. The firm can generally have pallets delivered to depots within two days in England, and three days for the rest of the UK, an ability which gives customers the luxury of ordering at short notice should the need arise.

The company's Market Division occupies the majority of Manchester's New Smithfield Market Fish Building, and supplies walk-in customers from 2.30am to 8.30am. Local caterers, public houses, Home Delivery companies and members of the public are supplied with a large range of wet, frozen, exotic and smoked fish.

The Wholesale Division of J. Sykes & Sons supplies full and mixed pallet quantities of frozen seafood to buying groups and individual companies, such as wholesalers, foodservice distributors, sandwich manufacturers and fish merchants.

Daily deliveries of fresh fish start at 4am, straight after the market opens, and fish is waiting for fryers when they arrive at their premises in the morning.

Frozen products for fish and chip shops are sourced from all over the world, every one of which is thoroughly tested before being distributed to the fish frying trade.

With some 70 staff working for Sykes' and annual sales of an astonishing £43 million their seafood business is rapidly expanding.

The company has enjoyed a long and illustrious past. With its long and established history of integrity when dealing with both suppliers and customers, its emphasis on quality and service and its long serving and loyal staff Sykes Seafoods is looking forward to a prosperous future.

As for J Sykes & Sons' status as a genuine family firm, that looks set to continue far into the future, with the fifth generation of the family as equally hooked on fish as their great great grandfather, the firm's founder, Joseph Sykes.

Left: A aerial view of the site in 1973.
Top: Inside the J Sykes & Sons premises in 2001.
Right: From left to right: Robert Sykes, Alexander Sykes (sons of David), Matthew Sykes (son of Martin), David Sykes and Martin Sykes.

WARTIME

When the Luftwaffe struck just before Christmas in 1940, the scene of devastation around Parker Street and Piccadilly was heartbreaking. Great warehouses, fine public buildings and handsome stores were laid to waste. Churches and hospitals, buildings that had no practical use in the war effort, were gutted as the indiscriminate bombing continued. Manchester lost 559 of its inhabitants, with thousands more suffering various degrees of injury. Nearly 2,000 houses were destroyed or damaged so badly that they had to be demolished. It was during these dark times that our emergency services and civil defence volunteers came into their own. Ignoring their own personal safety, the firefighters toiled round the clock in an effort to bring the flames under control. Fleets of ambulances ferried the injured to hospital and the Women's Voluntary Service, Red Cross and St John Ambulance volunteers organised blankets, mobile refreshment stations and anything they could think of that would provide support. The German assault on our towns and cities began in earnest after the Battle of Britain. There had been air raids before, but nothing could compare with the onslaught that came after our brave pilots beat the might of the enemy's air force during August 1940. That success blunted Hitler's invasion plans, but he wrought a vicious revenge on the civilian population thereafter.

Left: John Betjeman once wrote, 'Come friendly bombs and rain on Slough' to show his dislike of the appearance of the Berkshire town. He would not have been so sardonic if he had lived through the bombing raids that hit Manchester in the early 1940s while he was safe in Dublin. The first sirens sounded during the summer of 1940 and sporadic raids continued throughout August and into the autumn. After neighbouring Liverpool was hit late in the year it was inevitable that Manchester would not escape a major, concerted offensive. On 22 December the German Luftwaffe began its onslaught in one of the fiercest raids of the Blitz. Many of the city's fine Victorian buildings were hit in a 48-hour offensive, including the Free Trade Hall, the Royal Exchange, Manchester Cathedral, Piccadilly Gardens and Corporation Street. Baxendales, a huge hardware store that stocked everything from wheelbarrows to agricultural equipment, was obliterated from Miller Street. Fire crews worked for two days to control the flames and by 3am on Christmas Eve the fire appeared to be contained, but a sudden change in wind direction caused sparks to fly up and the fire spread quickly out of control once more. It was not until the afternoon of Christmas Day that all of the fires were brought under control.

Below: Looking like some form of monsters from 'Dr Who', this band of men from the decontamination squad put their backs into it as they swept and hosed down the streets around the Old Shambles. Dressed in protective clothing and sporting the gas masks that, thankfully, became redundant, they worked hard to make sure that no noxious substances had been included in the bombs that fell on the city in December 1940. Despite the wanton destruction around them, the Old Wellington Inn and Sinclair's Oyster Bar emerged damaged but largely intact. The pub dated from 1552, in Tudor times, but was moved from this site in 1974 during the city centre remodelling and the creation of the Arndale Centre. The entire structure was raised by 4ft 9in and moved into Shambles Square. In 1996 the building sustained considerable damage as a result of the IRA bomb that devastated the city centre. Restoration was complete by February 1997 and after dismantlement the building was moved 300 metres towards Manchester Cathedral. The pub reopened in November 1999. Sinclair's dates from 1720 and still serves its succulent oysters, along with substantial pub meals. In centuries gone by, The Shambles stood on what was then the main route from London to Carlisle, so it was a major stopping off point for all kinds of ravenous travellers and traders heading in and out of the city.

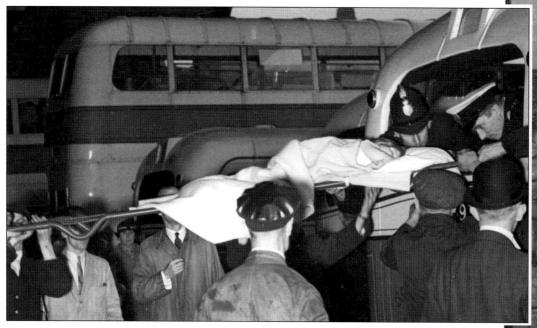

Above: One of the mobile first aid posts used in Manchester during the 1939-45 war is seen here in operation. An injured child is here being moved via the rear window of the converted single decker bus. Presumably, she had damaged her spine and had to be kept as immobile as possible. Whether this is a training routine or was shot for real is not clear, but such initiative and ingenuity was part and parcel of the Air Raid Precaution Service during those awful years. Sadly, those brave ladies with the lamps were not immune from danger. High explosive shows no mercy, nor does it discriminate between the young and the elderly, the hero and the villain. Such was the case during one of the heaviest raids on the Manchester area that took place just after midnight on Whit Sunday, 1 June 1941. Destruction and loss of life was on a very heavy scale that night. It was during this concentrated 90 minute onslaught that 14 nurses were killed in the tragic incident at Salford Royal Infirmary when the hospital received a direct hit. The hospital that dated from 1830 had never witnessed such devastation. A plaque was later erected in honour of those who were killed, but no-one there ever forgot the night that the Luftwaffe showed its true mettle in bombing such an establishment. There were many other casualties and deaths in different parts of Manchester and Salford during that particular raid, but few left such poignant memories.

Right: The first bomb to fall in the vicinity came down on Salford in late July 1940. Although there were further sporadic raids, Manchester was largely untouched until the enemy brought an unwelcome Christmas present later in the year. Cannon Street was just one section of the city that became a smoking ruin. From dusk to dawn there was seldom a period of more than two minutes when a bomb could not be heard falling. The centre of the city bore witness to the savagery of the attack. In the first hours of the attack wave upon wave of 25 or more bombers in quick succession scattered hundreds of bombs of all types over a wide area. Brilliant moonlight was not sufficient for the German airmen who dropped flares and incendiary bombs to light up the scene soon to be bathed in a great red glow. The barrage from the ground defences never slackened and for most of the night the raiders were kept at a great height from which accurate bombing was impossible. However, most of the aviators were not too concerned about where the planes dropped their payloads. If whatever target had been selected was not easily identifiable, then so be it. They opened their bomb doors and scooted off back home as quickly as they could, leaving a trail of carnage behind them.

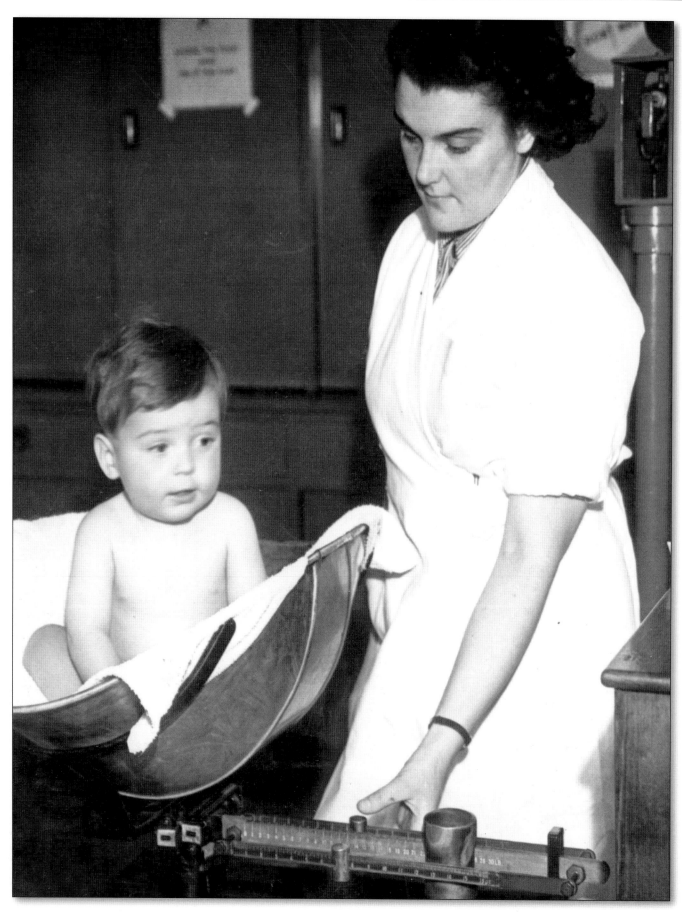

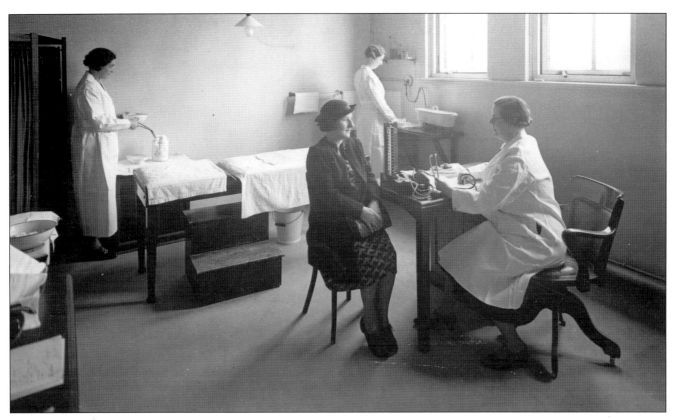

Both pages: It was possibly the acute wartime shortages of food and supplies which made doctors, health workers and mothers alike very aware of the health of the new generation, and children were carefully weighed, measured and immunised against the illnesses that had at one time meant disfigurement or even death *(facing page)*. A vaccine for polio, the scourge of former years which left behind its terrible mark of wasted and useless limbs, only came later, however. American scientist Jonas Edward Salk developed a vaccine in 1955, and an oral vaccine was produced in 1960. The vaccines brought the dreaded disease under control and today polio is rarely seen. On a day to day basis, vitamins were vital to the health of children, and long before the advent of the cod liver oil capsule, the recommended spoonful of cod liver oil was administered to the youngest children every day in schools and nurseries around the country during the 1940s. Children might have screwed up their noses at the fishy taste, but the nourishing cod liver oil went a long way towards keeping them

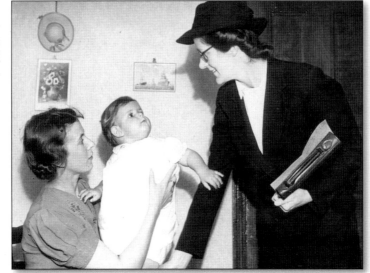

healthy. The vitamin-packed orange juice was far more palatable, and artful mothers would often use the orange juice as a bribe: no cod liver oil, no orange juice. Following hard on the heels of the oil, the juice took away the distinctive taste that was disliked by so many children. Ante-natal clinics did all they could to check on the diet, blood pressure and vitamin intake of mothers to be; our carefully posed photograph *(top)*, taken in an ante-natal clinic in the 1930s, records at least the cleanliness and tidiness that was to their great credit. And when the tiny new citizen finally arrived, there were health visitors to pay friendly calls on families in their homes to check on the health and happiness of mothers and babies *(left)*. National Dried Milk for babies was also made available to mothers, and before today's push towards natural feeding NDM was for decades very much in vogue. We need to remember that at the time of these photographs the National Health service did not exist, and in fact the NHS only came into operation after World War II in July 1948.

EVENTS OF THE
1940s

WHAT'S ON?

In wartime Britain few families were without a wireless set. It was the most popular form of entertainment, and programmes such as ITMA, Music While You Work and Workers' Playtime provided the people with an escape from the harsh realities of bombing raids and ration books. In 1946 the BBC introduced the Light Programme, the Home Service and the Third Programme, which gave audiences a wider choice of listening.

GETTING AROUND

October 1948 saw the production of Britain's first new car designs since before the war. The Morris Minor was destined for fame as one of the most popular family cars, while the four-wheel-drive Land Rover answered the need for a British-made off-road vehicle.

The country was deeply in the red, however, because of overseas debts incurred during the war. The post-war export drive that followed meant that British drivers had a long wait for their own new car.

SPORTING CHANCE

American World Heavyweight Boxing Champion Joe Louis, who first took the title back in 1937, ruled the world of boxing during the 1930s and 40s, making a name for himself as unbeatable. Time after time he successfully defended his title against all comers, finally retiring in 1948 after fighting an amazing 25 title bouts throughout his boxing career. Louis died in 1981 at the age of 67.

Bread was not rationed during World War II, but queues for the staff of life show that it was in short supply at times. Meat, butter and eggs all required coupons for their purchase, but that did not mean that they were always available. When word went round that a particular butcher had just got some chops in, housewives made a swift journey to his counter, only to find that everyone else had the same idea. At one time, we were rationed to half an egg per person a week. That conjured up some amusing cartoons suggesting how that egg could be divided. In May 1946 bread actually made it onto the list of commodi-

ties placed on the ration list. Europe faced a food shortage, especially as there were some 30 million Germans facing starvation as that country's agricultural infrastructure had collapsed. There were not too many Britons who had much sympathy with the plight of their former enemies. On 15 August 1945, these women might have grumbled about the length of the queue that they were in and the dark bread they had to swallow, but there were smiles on their faces. Victory in Japan had been secured on the previous day after Emperor Hirihito unconditionally surrendered in the wake of the atomic bombs unleashed on Hiroshima and Nagasaki.

Above: An old wind up gramophone was requisitioned from someone's front room. We had not partied since the Coronation in 1937, so a real old knees up was in order and Mother Brown had a right royal time celebrating the end of hostilities in May 1945. Children looked on with a mixture of amusement and astonishment as mums and grannies let down their hair. Of course, there were not too many young men around to join in the festivities. Most were still in uniform and some were still fighting the Japanese forces in the Far East, a campaign that still had three months to run. Then there were those men who would never come back. Their widows and mums shed a quiet tear that the street party was also a memorial to them. For each one who looked forward to the day she would be reunited with her loved one there was another who knew that hers lay in a foreign field. Even so, they shared the happiness of their neighbours as flags and bunting left suddenly appeared out of boxes and were flown from lampposts or stretched across the street. Mums in their pinnies used up a week's ration of sugar, eggs, butter and flour to make tasty goodies for the little ones to enjoy in the biggest series of parties the nation has ever seen.

Below: When the war was over at last, just about every street in the country looked like this one. Out came the bunting. Up went the union flags. Everywhere was festooned with symbols of patriotism on VE Day as the whole country erupted with a mixture of joy and relief. After nearly six years of fighting the Germans, it was all over. The desperate days of drabness, shortages, blitzes, death and despair were temporarily forgotten and in their wake came a blaze of multi- coloured flags, fireworks and floodlights. Civilians linked arms with servicemen and whooped at the tops of their voices. Complete strangers hugged and kissed each other. Huge congas and hokey-cokeys were danced around the statues in town centres. There was dancing in the street, whistles blowing and trumpets sounding. Bands struck up 'Rule Britannia' and crowds warbled about bluebirds and the white cliffs of Dover. Trestle tables were dragged out of church halls and schoolrooms. They were set out in the back streets as neighbours mucked in together for impromptu street parties. A week's ration was blown in just one afternoon. But, what the matter? We had something worth celebrating. Somehow little buns, sandwiches and jugs of lemonade appeared. Children made party hats from bits of paper and card that had escaped the salvage drives.

SHOPPING SPREE

Lewis's store that was in business from 1877 to 2001 on the corner of Market Street and Piccadilly was a favourite meeting place for a girl and boy who were 'walking out' together in 1957 if they came from different suburbs in Manchester. The store arcade was just around the corner from the bus stands and many a young man waited patiently for his sweetheart to arrive on a Saturday night. Then it was off to one of the burgeoning coffee bars that had a juke box where the couple could sit at a table over a couple of frothy cups and gaze into each other's eyes. Tab Hunter's 'Young love' described their feelings for each other quite admirably. However, Tommy Steele's 'Rock with the caveman' or Jerry Lee Lewis and 'Great balls of fire' would be the pounding background. These were hardly messages of romance, but youngsters preferred such raw sounds to the wishy-washy 'Around the world' by Ronnie Hilton. Couples would move on to spend the evening dancing at the Ritz Ballroom or on the back row at any of a large number of cinemas in the city. When it came time to say goodbye, they walked back to the bus station, shared a goodnight kiss and arranged to meet next week, same time, same place. This was witnessed by Sir Robert Peel from the plinth where his statue had stood since the middle of the previous century

Below: The buildings that stood in this part of the city around Market Street, Cross Street and Corporation Street were due to be obliterated in the 1958 redevelopment plans. Some of the businesses were none too happy about it. Beaty Brothers had the 'Premises to be Demolished' sign up and Prossers' pawnbroker shop made its feelings very clear with 'Forced out after 50 years' on its façade. Not everyone shed a tear for the passing of the

Above: In 1958 this corner of Rochdale Road and Victoria Avenue in Blackley was part of the main A664 route from the city centre that ran on into Middleton and Rochdale before joining the A58 trans Pennine route to Ripponden and Halifax. Today, links to the nearby M60 orbital motorway, M66 to Bury and M62 to Yorkshire offer a variety of faster routes out of the area. Blackley is pronounced 'Blake-ley', a source of confusion to outsiders, and takes its name from an old English word that meant 'clearing in a dark wood'. In medieval times deer and wolves roamed the area and it was a popular hunting location. Blackley Hall stood at the junction of Rochdale Road and Middleton Road from Tudor times and was the home of the Assheton family, local wealthy landowners and philanthropists. The Assheton Arms pub in Middleton town centre continues to keep the family name alive. The Hall was demolished in the early 19th century. Blackley estate was once owned by the Byrom family, from whom the poet Lord Byron was descended with the help of a slight name change. In this photograph, the Avenue Cinema was showing 'The Little Hut', a poor Hollywood attempt to make a film of a French farce about a man, his wife and her lover who are shipwrecked and marooned on a desert island. Its stars could not be faulted as they were amongst the biggest box office draws around, but Stewart Granger, David Niven and Ava Gardner have had better roles. The Avenue was part of the Snape and Ward circuit that included the Carlton in Clayton and the Fourways in Moston.

pawnbroker as there were mixed feelings about followers of this profession. Borrowing money with an agreed (however high) rate of interest against a pledge or pawn has been happening for thousands of years. Although the main retail business started with the Lombard goldsmith-brokers in London in the 16th century and reached its peak in the middle of the 19th century, the custom started at a very early date at the highest level. Even our monarchs turned to the pawnbroker when

short of a bob or two. King Henry III, in about 1240, pledged a valuable 'Image of the Virgin' to obtain money to pay his officers of the Crown. The famous sign of three balls indicating a pawnbroker establishment to show their trade derived from the Lombard goldsmiths who came originally from the Medicis in Italy. Three blue circular discs formed part of the Medici coat of arms. To show the association with goldsmiths the blue discs subsequently became gold balls.

EVENTS OF THE 1930s

WHAT'S ON?

In this heyday of the cinema, horrified audiences were left gasping at the sight of Fay Wray in the clutches of the giant ape in the film 'King Kong', released in 1933. Very different but just as gripping was the gutsy 1939 American Civil War romance 'Gone with the Wind'. Gable's parting words, 'Frankly, my dear, I don't give a damn' went down in history.

GETTING AROUND

At the beginning of the decade many believed that the airship was the transport of the future. The R101 airship, however, loaded with thousands of cubic metres of hydrogen, crashed in France on its maiden flight in 1930. Forty-eight passengers and crew lost their lives. In 1937 the Hindenburg burst into flames - the entire disaster caught on camera and described by a distraught reporter. The days of the airship were numbered.

SPORTING CHANCE

The black American Jesse Owens broke a brilliant four world records in the 1936 Olympic Games in Berlin, thumbing the nose to Adolf Hitler's dreams of Aryan superiority. In a petty display Hitler walked out of the stadium and 'took his bat home'; later he refused to have his photograph taken with the victorious Owens.

HOT OFF THE PRESS

The years of the 1930s saw Adolf Hitler's sickening anti-Jewish campaign echoed in the streets of Britain. On 19th October 1936 Oswald Mosley's 7,000-strong British Union of Fascists clashed head on with thousands of Jews and Communists in London, resulting in 80 people being injured in the ensuing battle. Mosley and his 'blackshirts' later rampaged through the streets beating up Jews and smashing the windows of their businesses. A dark day in our country's history.

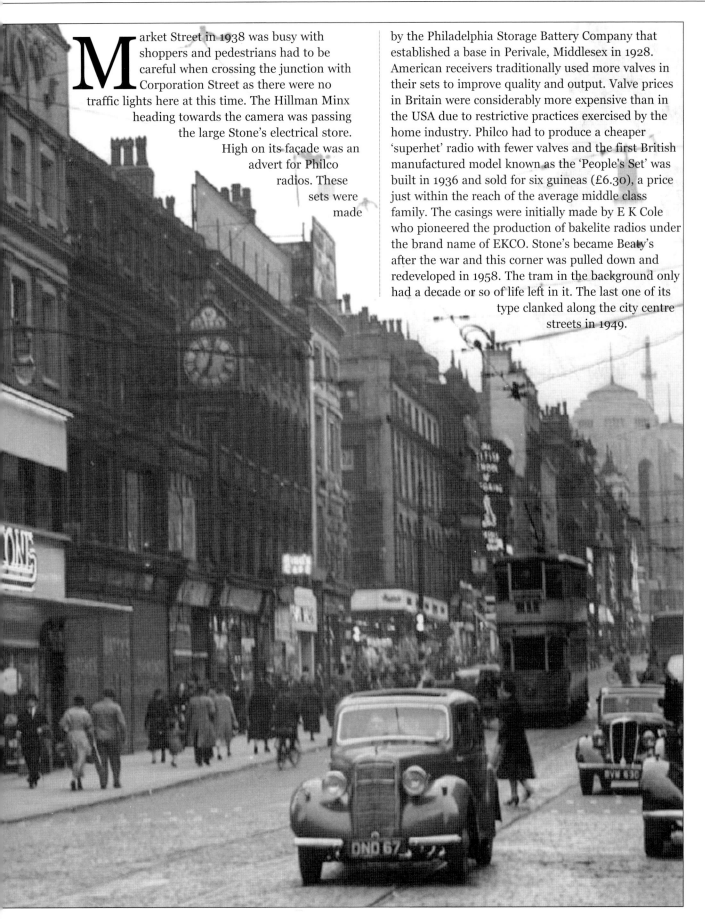

Market Street in 1938 was busy with shoppers and pedestrians had to be careful when crossing the junction with Corporation Street as there were no traffic lights here at this time. The Hillman Minx heading towards the camera was passing the large Stone's electrical store. High on its façade was an advert for Philco radios. These sets were made by the Philadelphia Storage Battery Company that established a base in Perivale, Middlesex in 1928. American receivers traditionally used more valves in their sets to improve quality and output. Valve prices in Britain were considerably more expensive than in the USA due to restrictive practices exercised by the home industry. Philco had to produce a cheaper 'superhet' radio with fewer valves and the first British manufactured model known as the 'People's Set' was built in 1936 and sold for six guineas (£6.30), a price just within the reach of the average middle class family. The casings were initially made by E K Cole who pioneered the production of bakelite radios under the brand name of EKCO. Stone's became Beaty's after the war and this corner was pulled down and redeveloped in 1958. The tram in the background only had a decade or so of life left in it. The last one of its type clanked along the city centre streets in 1949.

TRANSPORT

Manchester Corporation trams and buses ran side by side for many years. In this 1946 photograph, taken from Lewis's department store looking across Piccadilly, examples of both can be seen. Public transport was at its height during this era. Petrol rationing restricted the number of miles that the private motorist could manage. Ownership of such vehicles was still for the minority as it would be at least another decade before the family saloon became a common sight on our roads. Consequently, we used double decker transport for our everyday needs in getting to work, travelling to school, going shopping or heading off into town for a night out.

Electrically operated trams first saw the light of day at the start of the last century. The first section of the reconstructed horse drawn tramway, between Albert Square and Cheetham Hill, was opened for electric traction on 7 June 1901. The full remodelling of the public transport system was completed by 1903 and the last horse trams within the city were phased out. Many small authorities now owned sections of tramway and it was agreed that Manchester would reconstruct these and lease them for operation. The first motor buses were trialled on some of the lightly used routes in the suburbs as early as 1906, though it was after the first world war that they really came into their own.

Above: Car parking was available at the side of Piccadilly on Parker Street in 1957. This was just one of the bomb sites that had never been redeveloped after the war. Large warehouses had once stood on and around here, but they were destroyed in late 1940. Staines Inlaid Linoleum, J Templeton and Co and Peel, Watson and Co were reduced to rubble as fires swept across Portland Street and beyond. It was a large price to pay for the motorists' peacetime convenience. However, they would not enjoy it for much longer. As the nation's economy began to boom, major reinvestment meant that open spaces were a thing of the past and office blocks and hotels soon swallowed up what spare land they could. New bays had just been fitted for the buses on Piccadilly and the landscape would take on a new vista in the 1960s with the building of the Piccadilly Plaza and its neighbours. Across on Mosley Street, though, there has been little change. Tenants may have come and gone, but the buildings largely remain. The advert for Mother's Pride has disappeared, but the company is still going strong as part of the Rank Hovis McDougall group. It made its first appearance in the north in 1936 and became a national brand in 1956. It was heavily advertised throughout the 1960s and 1970s, some of which won awards, including some that appeared during the 1974 general election. The punning lines included 'Support your local MP' and 'Meet your MP tonight'. Other famous adverts include 'I'm the Mother in Mothers Pride', featuring the voice over of Thora Hird, and Dusty Springfield as 'The Happy Knocker Upper'.

Below: The Kardomah was designed by Misha Black (1910-77) and its art deco styling helped make it one of the city's most popular coffee houses either side of the second world war. Ladies met there for a respite from a heavy day's shopping and swapped tales as they happily gossiped together. However, it was not just a dropping in place for the blue rinse brigade as, around 1950 when this photograph was taken, LS Lowry could often be found quietly sipping from a cup as he sat in a corner watching the world go by. He used to take it all in as he looked for inspiration for another matchstalk men and matchstalk cats and dogs style of painting. William Turner, another prolific painter of northern industrial and urban landscapes, also enjoyed the atmosphere of the Kardomah. Those requiring a stronger brew would enter the nearby Old Wellington Inn. The crowded scene in front of us was observed around Market Place, at the bottom of Market Street, within which were the Shambles or stalls. The Old Wellington Inn and the adjoining Sinclair's Oyster Bar were both rare survivors of pre-industrial Manchester. The former and older of the two had stood on this site since the 16th century. In 1971 the Old Wellington was jacked up and moved to its a site in Exchange Square on the edge of the Arndale Centre during redevelopment work that completely changed the nature of this part of the city.

The postwar view across Piccadilly bus station shows how dependent we were on public transport in those days. Horse drawn omnibuses had been introduced in the 19th century and by 1850 Manchester had 64 such vehicles. Tramways were laid and both steam and horse drawn cars made an appearance during the latter part of the 1800s. The Manchester Suburban Tramways Company was formed

in 1877 to build and operate its own lines. The original leases were signed in 1877 to run for a period of 21 years and were later to become very important determining factors in the introduction of municipal operations to the Manchester transport scene. On 17 May 1877, horse tramway operations began with a service between the Grove Inn on Bury New Road and Deansgate. The motor bus was introduced in the early 20th century and by the 1920s was becoming a serious rival to the tram. This section of the Manchester Corporation undertaking grew from 16 vehicles in 1923 to 51 in 1926. On Saturday nights the bus station was thronged with courting couples saying goodbye to one another as they got onto different buses to make their ways home. It is quirky now to see trams running through the area once again, considering that the original services in the city centre were wound up in 1949.

AT WORK

The ranks on Piccadilly were well used by passengers and buses in 1957. Public transport within the city went back over a century even then. John Greenwood, proprietor of the Pendleton Toll Gates, started a regular horse bus or coach service to Manchester's Market Street that first ran on New Year's Day 1824. The coach had room for eight passengers and operated three times a day. By the 1830s there were horsedrawn buses running from the rail terminus at Liverpool Road to Market Street and a service connecting Manchester and Stockport. Double deckers, drawn by three horses, were introduced in the 1850s. The city's first tram ran between the Grove Inn on Bury New Road and Deansgate. Electrification meant a reconstruction of the tramways and the first of the new form of tram went into service between Albert Square and Cheetham Hill on 7 June 1901. The last horse tram went in 1903. Motor buses were introduced three years later, but did not challenge the trams' supremacy until after the first world war. Although trolley-buses ran in Ramsbottom and Stockport from 1913, it took until 1938 before Manchester took them on board. Piccadilly bus station is something of a misnomer as it was really a collection of stands situated on a highway.

EVENTS OF THE 1950s

THE WORLD AT LARGE

Plans to develop the economies of member states into one common market came to fruition on 1st January 1958, when the EEC came into operation. The original members were France, Belgium, Luxembourg, The Netherlands, Italy, and West Germany. The Community became highly successful, achieving increased trade and prosperity across Western Europe while at the same time alleviating fear of war which lingered on after the end of World War II. Britain became a member in 1973.

ROYAL WATCH

King George VI's health had been causing problems since 1948, when he developed thrombosis. In 1951 the King - always a heavy smoker - became ill again, and was eventually found to be suffering from lung cancer. His left lung was removed in September of 1951. In January 1952 he waved Princess Elizabeth and Prince Philip off on their tour of Africa; they were never to see him again. The King died on 5th February 1952.

MELODY MAKERS

Few teenage girls could resist the blatant sex-appeal of 'Elvis the Pelvis', though their parents were scandalised at the moody Presley's provocatively gyrating hips. The singer took America and Britain by storm with such hits as 'Jailhouse Rock', 'All Shook Up' and 'Blue Suede Shoes'. The rhythms of Bill Haley and his Comets, Buddy Holly, Chuck Berry, and Roy Orbison (who had a phenomenal three-octave voice) turned the 1950s into the Rock 'n' Roll years.

Left: A woman's work is never done. This was doubly true during the second world war. When the men marched, sailed or flew off into the distance it was their womenfolk who filled the void. They donned overalls, dungarees, boiler suits and drivers' uniforms as they turned lathes, harvested the crops, operated heavy machinery and drove lorries. In addition to this, there was a home to run and mouths to feed. These women worked in an ordnance factory, turning out shell caps. Every so often they would mark one with a message, such as 'this one's for you Adolf' or something a bit fruitier. Women not only saw this work as 'doing their bit' for the war effort, but as a chance to get away from the kitchen sink and rid themselves of the stereotype of existing purely as a baby factory, cook and cleaner. After the war, many women were not prepared to abandon the jobs and careers they had committed themselves to for up to six years. Those men who could not accept that changes had come while they had been away found themselves in dispute with those same loved ones for whom they had been fighting. Whilst other couples were reunited and celebrated by creating the baby boomer period, elsewhere divorce figures went through the roof.

Above: The fruit stall in The Shambles was typical of many that traded here in the early 1960s. In a part of the city where a slaughterhouse once stood, shoppers enjoyed the intimacy of dealing with individual stallholders. This one, in her traditional flowered pinnie, had probably traded from here for many years, but all that was to change when the bulldozers moved in. The swinging sixties were times when it was not just buildings that took on a whole new look. Youth started to have its say as we saw the immediate postwar baby boomers approach adulthood. Having grown up during the austere years of the late 40s and early 50s, these young people had money in their pockets and demanded a right to be heard. They did not want to replicate the dress, style, actions and attitudes of their parents and grandparents. After all, what good had it done them? The first half of the century had seen two world wars, the depression years of high unemployment and restrictions and rationing. That was not good enough for the new breed and change was not just expected but demanded. Young people felt that the old values were not to be respected and they imposed some new ones of their own. It is amusing to think that those radicals are now grandparents and, no doubt, tut-tutting about 'young people today'!

Voith - A world of paper

Voith Paper is one of the world's leading companies in paper technology. Almost a third of the world's paper is produced on Voith Paper plants. Perhaps even more interestingly all UK banknotes pass through one of Voith's 'calenders' to give the paper its final finish.

Some 34,000 people are employed by the company throughout the globe. And a vital part of that global network is to be found at Middleton just outside Manchester. The company's Apex Works enjoys a multi-million pound annual turnover producing 'rolls' and 'calenders' for the paper industry together with extensive service activities.

Though the name Voith Paper Ltd is a relatively recent arrival in Middleton the business in fact traces its origins in the area back more than century to the well-remembered firm of Hunt & Moscrop, which at its peak had some 600 employees.

Above: Founders of Hunt & Moscrop, Edward W Hunt (left) and Walter Moscrop. *Below:* Early promotional literature dated 1906. *Right:* A report by Edward Hunt addressed to his father, 1907.

The company of Hunt & Moscrop was founded in 1906 as a partnership by Edward Wilson Hunt and Walter Moscrop.

Originally situated at the Central Iron Works, Middleton the firm specialised in the manufacture of high quality machinery for the bleaching, dyeing and finishing of textile piece goods.

In 1908 Edward W Hunt decided to start manufacturing 'calender bowls' in a small way, and a small bowl-making plant was installed to manufacture these items for sale to paper-makers, textile finishers and embossers.

The next two years saw steady progress. In 1910 the partnership was converted into a private limited company, with Edward W Hunt having the controlling interest. The

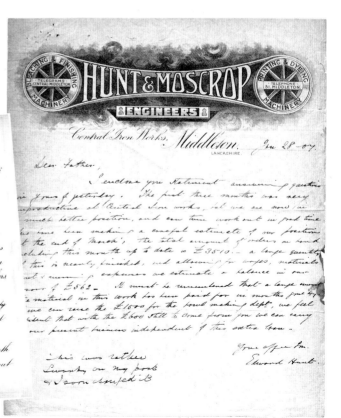

Hunt & Moscrop Ltd held an interest of about 40 per cent in the new company, but Edward W Hunt and his family retained controlling interest of both firms.

The founder's son, Edward Francis (known as Francis) Hunt, was appointed to the board of both companies in 1928, the year in which Hunt & Moscrop began manufacturing machinery specifically for the paper industry in addition to the textile industry.

Young Francis had served a full practical and technical apprenticeship in engineering prior to his appointment.

In 1934 Francis Hunt was appointed Managing Director of both Hunt & Moscrop and the Middleton Bowl Works: his father retired in 1936.

Young Francis travelled widely: he visited the USA to secure the British Empire Rights for the manufacture and distribution of patented American machinery for singeing cloth prior to bleaching; this would prove to be a highly profitably line. In 1937 he also bought and equipped the Junction Iron Works at Middleton Junction solely for the manufacture of drying machinery and heaters.

year was also to be marked by the company acquiring the British manufacturing rights for the Gantt Continuous Bleaching Machine which revolutionised the system of cotton bleaching, making the process continuous.

Manufacture of textile machinery was discontinued during the first world war, due to government work, by 1919 however, the company had resumed the manufacture of textile machinery, and the policy of supplying first-class machinery was continued.

In 1920 Edward W Hunt created a new private company, Middleton Bowl Works, Ltd. The new business was to concentrate on the manufacture of calender bowls – it would be the largest bowl-making plant in Britain, and provided a key component for the production of 'super calenders' for the paper industry. A portion of Central Iron Works was rented to Middleton Bowl Works, Ltd and additional plant installed.

The manufacture of drying machines began in 1935. The following year the company obtained the services of John Sharpe who was soon appointed to the Board of both companies. John Sharpe was an expert in the design and manufacture of drying machinery and extended-surface air heaters and coolers. With John Sharpe's advice this side of the business expanded rapidly.

Top left: A Hunt & Moscrop brochure of the 'Gantt' system. Top right: Apex Mill, destroyed by fire in the 1940s which eventually became the site of Apex Works. Above: Former Managing Directors Edward F Hunt (left) and John Sharpe.

In 1939 the firm was asked to take contracts for defence work, and from 1940 to 1942 half of the plant was engaged

in such activities. By 1942 almost the entire Central Works was occupied with government contracts turning out tank parts and brake gear for heavy vehicles.

During 1942 Francis Hunt was asked to also take on contracts for gun recoil gear and field gun transporters. He realised that in order to take on this work further premises would be required, and he was able to purchase the Apex Works, which adjoined the Junction Works.

The Apex Works was soon equipped with new, modern machinery throughout. In 1943 Francis Hunt was asked to take on even more government contracts; in response he decide to build a new modern factory alongside Apex Works. The new factory was finished and in production by 1944.

Meanwhile, during the whole of the early 1940s, the Junction Works continued to turn out drying machinery and heaters in increasing numbers, many of which went to other factories to help increase national production in many different fields.

Business founder Edward W Hunt resigned as Chairman of both companies in 1945 and Francis Hunt was now appointed Chairman and Managing Director.

That year John Sharpe designed and patented novel machinery for the high speed drying of wallpaper and coated paper. The new machines were a great commercial

and technical success, and large contracts for them were soon being received.

After the war EF Hunt decided on a policy of redesigning the whole range of products on the most up-to-date lines and to strike out for world trade.

Because of the great demand further extension was necessary. It was decide to build a completely new modern

Top: Edward F Hunt in the workshop.
Above: A huge Swimming Roll destined for the USSR is viewed by Jim Sharpe (centre), Managing Director at the time, former Directors Norman Prior (left) and Geoff Hill.

erection shop and offices at the Apex Works. After completing the new buildings the whole of the production of Hunt & Moscrop Ltd was transferred to Apex and Junction Works. Central Works was allocated exclusively to Middleton Bowl Works, Ltd.

The new erection shop was built to an exceptional height to allow for the erection of the very tall machines required in the papermaking industry.

Middleton Bowl Works Ltd now installed additional bowl-making plant, which was capable of doubling production. The year to June 1946, the first year after the end of the war, showed a poor financial result because of the reconstruction and re-equipment of the works. By the end of the year however, production was increasing month by month, and by 1948 the monthly output was above eight times that of 1938. Orders were now being received from not only Europe but also from Asia, Africa, and both North and South America.

By the following year the combined net profits of the two firms before director's remuneration or taxation was the then huge sum of more than £ 60,000.

During 1948 EF Hunt personally made an extended visit to both Canada and the USA looking at new machinery and inventions: as a result he secured the sole British rights for a new American machine much in demand by the woollen and worsted trades. New machinery was being introduced not only for drying wool but also the latest in manmade fibres.

Edward Francis Hunt held the post as managing director until his death in 1958; his son, Edward W Hunt, was still only a teenager at this time. He joined the company as a trainee in the factory, working through the ranks to take over as MD from John Sharpe in the 1970s.

During the 1960s a license agreement was obtained from a German company Edward Kuesters GmbH to manufacture the 'Swimming Roll'. This was a key event. The first roll was produced in 1964. When the licence agreement expired the company was free to market the product worldwide: this in turn led to larger rolls and even more orders. For a time these would be the company's main product. At its height in 1988 some 195 of these rolls were sold in a single year.

But what exactly is a 'Swimming Roll?'

The whole machine that puts the finish on paper is a called a 'calender'. When a calender is designed to produce very high quality paper it is called a 'super calender'.

Calenders in turn contain a series of steel cylinders called 'rolls'. And the most critical of the rolls in a calender is the 'swimming roll'.

A 'swimming roll' is a hollow cylinder made with chambers to receive oil under pressure at just the right places and times so that any flexing or distortion whilst rolling paper is balanced out, ensuring that the paper finish is kept exactly the same throughout its full width and length.

Left: A Supercalender for Donacona.

The largest 'swimming roll' ever made in Manchester was a 30-foot long giant made for export to the Soviet Union.

In 1963, another member of the family, Geoffrey Hunt joined the company. He was to hold a number of Director posts before leaving the Group in 1988 to set up his own consultancy company.

By the early 1970s Hunt & Moscrop was made up of nine companies - each with its own organisation but with manufacturing facilities often integrated. In addition to the holding company these were: H&M Ltd, Middleton Bowl Works Ltd, Hunt Heat Exchangers Ltd, H&M Canada Ltd, Whitehead & Poole Ltd, Turnbull & Scott (Engineers) Ltd, Johnson-Hunt Ltd and Chemical & Thermal Engineering Ltd.

The demise of the textile industry in the 1970s would lead to the end of the company's textile division in the mid-1980s when the remaining aspects of that business were sold off.

Also in the 1980s the whole of the Hunt & Moscrop Group was bought by Biwater Ltd.

In 1985 Hunt & Moscrop Apex Works was bought by the German company Kleinewefers, which lead to the transfer of certain H&M products to the German owners including Supercalenders.

The transfer of business, together with new advances in the application of synthetic (plastic) type coverings on the rollers would eventually lead to the demise of bowl manufacture.

In the late 1980s, H&M purchased the rights to the Farrel Swimming Roll business in the USA. A sales office in Atlanta was established under the name of Hunt & Moscrop Inc. With the vision and drive of Geoffrey Sword (then Sales Director, later to become joint Managing Director) this provided the springboard to a substantial increase in sales, including calenders in North America.

In 1990 the company gained the Queen's Award for Export Achievement. In one sense this was inevitable: the company had by then become part of an international enterprise.

Further mergers and takeovers would soon follow. In the early 1990s Kleinewefers was taken over by Sulzer Escher Wyss. In the early 1990s Sulzer Escher Wyss in turn merged with another German firm, JM Voith AG, to become Voith

Top: A Hunt & Moscrop Supercalender.
Above: Edward W Hunt receiving the Queen's Award.

Voith - A world of paper

Over the following decades the small German firm would build many more machines for the papermaking industry. By its 25th anniversary the firm had over 300 employees. By the company's hundredth anniversary in 1967 it could boast 1,000 workers employed manufacturing a wide range of machines used for many industrial purposes.

Voith is certainly a name to be reckoned with when it comes to paper production. Following an unproblematic world record run, the previously unachievable limit of 2,000 metres per minute was exceeded on a Voith PM 1 machine in Hürth, Germany. Standard newsprint was produced at a speed of 2,010 m/min over a period of several hours.

During all the corporate changes Edward W Hunt, grandson of the company founder, had remained with the firm. In 2001 however, his retirement marked the end of one era and the beginning of the next when the new management team of Andrew Regan (Managing Director) and Nigel Ashworth (Engineering and Manufacturing Director) took control of the company.

Today one of the main focus of business in the United Kingdom is roll and fibre systems service. The largest market for capital machinery sales is now China though with sales going to paper mills across the world.

As for the future Voith, in Middleton and across the globe, is looking to develop even more hi-tech machinery for the paper industry whilst continuing to look at related industries where its products might be utilised. Diversification of products and services will be the keys to survival and growth in the 21st century.

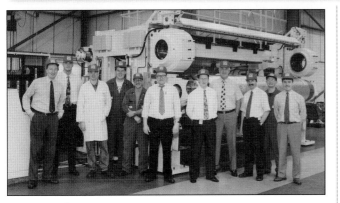

Sulzer Papertechnology leading to what had been Hunt & Moscrop becoming Voith Sulzer Finishing Ltd.

In 2000 JM Voith AG took over the controlling interest in Voith Sulzer Papertechnology and the company became today's Voith Paper Ltd.

Despite its vast global presence today the Voith company had humble origins. The business is named after Johann Matthäeus Voith (1803-1874). In 1825 at the age of 22 Johann took charge of his father's locksmiths workshop, at that time employing just five workers.

Five years later Johann Voith became involved in the construction of a papermaking machine being made by Johann Widmann from Heilbronn for the Rau and Voelter paper mill in Heidenheim.

Top: *An aerial view of the factory.*
Above: *The company is ready to deliver its first Ecosoft modular calender.* *Right:* *Pictured in 2001 L-R: Andrew Regan, Managing Director, Vernon Holt, Director (retired in 2001) and Nigel Ashworth, Engineering and Manufacturing Director.*

William Hulme's Grammar School - 'Trusting, but minding whom'

S upposedly the best days of our lives, our school-days were certainly the longest, since most of us could not wait for the bell to end each one of them!

In times past many of us stayed on at our local school only until the age of just 14 before leaving for the world of work. Other, somewhat younger, readers may have attended a 'Secondary Modern' or a brand new Comprehensive school. Still others may have passed their eleven-plus and gone to a Grammar school. And some readers will have attended a school which can trace its history back to the Victorian era, and its origins to events which occurred three centuries ago – Manchester's William Hulme's Grammar School.

Today William Hulme's in the North West of England is an independent co-educational day school incorporating a junior school, senior school and sixth form, situated in Manchester, close to the city centre.

William Hulme's has a history of excellent academic achievement and it strives to continue that tradition.

Each pupil is encouraged and supported in a caring, disciplined and happy community. Staff set high academic standards and offer a broad curriculum at all key stages. Pupils enjoy much success at GCSE and A level.

To balance the demands of academic work a range of activities and visits are offered to pupils, widening their horizons and developing their sense of responsibility and self-esteem.

William died in 1691, having left an enormous philanthropic bequest, and was buried in the Hulme Chapel of the Collegiate Church in Manchester, which had been largely built by his ancestors.

In his will William left provision for the foundation of 'exhibitions' or grants for four students to study for Bachelor of Arts degrees at Brasenose College. The income from this charity was originally £64 a year, which came from rents and dues on William's many outlying properties at Heaton Norris, Denton, Ashton-under-Lyne, Reddish, Harwood in Bolton, and in Manchester.

But when a school takes its name from an individual it begs the question 'just who was William Hulme?'

William Hulme (1631- 1691) was the founder of the William Hulme Charity. He lived at Hulme Hall (later Broadstone Hall) in Reddish, Stockport.

Very little is known about William's life except that he owned two other large properties in the region: one at Withingreave Hall in Withy Grove, Manchester, and another at Outwood near Prestwich.

Probably educated in Manchester, William was brought up by an uncle, after his father had died when he was just 11 years old. Opinions differ as to his adult life - some maintain that he followed a career at Law after attending Brasenose College in Oxford; others believe that he lived the life of a country gentleman. What we do know with certainty is that he held the position of Justice of the Peace for Kearsley near Bolton, where his wife Elizabeth had grown up.

The premature and tragic death of his beloved only son, was however to deeply affect William Hulme in later life, and he was determined to make some charitable provision for young boys.

Over the years, with the growth of Manchester, the value, and income, from the original Hulme estate grew to such an extent that it became necessary on several occasions to change the scope of his bequest by Act of Parliament. In 1881, the Trustees of the charity were empowered to build schools in Manchester, Oldham and Bury.

The Trustees also founded a Hall of Residence for students at Manchester University, made annual grants to the University itself and to the Manchester High School for Girls. The exhibitions at Brasenose College were increased from four to twenty.

In 1881 the Trustees agreed to build a new school in Manchester. A site for it was bought off Alexandra Road between Alexandra Park and Wilbraham Road. At that time Spring Bridge Road was nothing more than a dirty lane petering out on the school site.

The new school was designed to accommodate 400 boys with ample space for playgrounds, gymnasium and cricket fields. A headmaster, Mr Joseph Hall was appointed on an annual salary of £150, plus a capitation fee of £2 for every boy admitted to the school.

The school opened on 26th January 1887 with sixty-four boys. One Bernard Muth claimed to be the first pupil to step over the threshold. His devotion to the school would

Facing page top left: William Hulme's Grammar School, circa 1920. Left: The School's 1927-1928 lacrosse team in Manchester. Above: Chemistry lesson in 1927.

be evidenced by the fact that one of his last appearances at the school, before his death in 1965 at the age of 88, was when he played alongside his grandson in the school orchestra.

Few would ever forget the school's Latin motto 'Fide sed cui vide' – a punning witticism on the founder's name – 'Trust but mind whom'.

And if the motto were an insufficient reminder of whose bounty was ultimately behind the school's existence there was also the school prayer:

'O Lord, the resurrection and the life of them that believe, to be praised as well as those that live as in those that are departed: we give thee thanks for William Hulme, of whose bounty this school was founded and endowed, for William Roberts, Edward Donner and others our benefactors, past and present, by whose beneficence we are here maintained for the further attaining of Godliness and learning: beseeching thee to grant that we, well using to thy glory these Thy gifts, may rise again to eternal life with those that are departed in the faith of Christ: through Christ our Lord. Amen.'

Down the many decades since the school first opened its doors thousands upon thousands of pupils have received their education at 'William Hulme' taking away with them at the end of their schooldays not only well-earned examination certificates but also memories which last a lifetime.

No-one and nothing can ever erase those memories: teachers we loved or hated, school dinners; ink wells and blotting paper; the smells of chalk dust and changing rooms; bad things such as the cane, and good things such as sporting and academic triumphs. Laughter and tears. Friends made for life.

Though proud of their high academic standards present pupils looking back on their own time at school will no doubt also find their thoughts dwelling as much if not more on the remarkable range of supplementary activities offered by the school.

For example many pupils down the years have joined the school's combined cadet force, spending time at the annual Central Camp together with contingents from a dozen other schools experiencing live firing, military and survival skills in the Highlands of Scotland.

Others may retain fond memories of participating in the school's dramatic productions or being a part of the choir or concert band.

Perhaps school trips to foreign countries will also form part of the happy clutch of memories which will live with former pupils forever. On a trip to France in 2005 a large group of pupils visited Northern France, in the process not only learning how to make French bread but also visiting the historic site of the battle of Agincourt. Another group visited Barcelona in Spain, and yet another Austria.

Modern languages have become increasingly important in the present era and William Hulme's is at the forefront of language teaching. In 2005 a brand new state-of-the-art digital languages laboratory was opened at the school by Ivan Lewis MP Economic Secretary to the Treasury.

The Member of Parliament however was far from big the only prominent visitor to the school in 2005. On Friday 13th May the school hosted a visit by their Royal Highnesses the Earl and Countess of Wessex. Also visiting the school were the Lord and Lady Mayoress of Manchester, the Vice Lord Lieutenant, the High Sheriff and local MP Sir Gerald Kaufman.

Today under the leadership of headmaster Stephen Patriarca the William Hulme's Grammar School combines the values and standards of a traditional grammar school education with a modern, co-educational and international dimension which parents, pupils and staff believe provides unparalleled preparation for the world ahead.

This page: School photographs from 1953 (above) and 2006.

Williams Motor Company – Always delivering a high quality of service

I n Manchester today the name of the Williams Motor Company is synonymous with BMW, MINI and Land Rover. But the Williams name is far from new: the business has a long and rich history in the area.

Founded by John Henry Williams in 1909, the Williams Wheelwright Works started out repairing horse-drawn vehicles for the London and North Western Railways from premises in Manchester's Cornbrook. Now, a century later, the company has expanded to include ten dealerships across the North West employing hundreds of people and selling thousands of vehicles each year.

No doubt at the time he began his fledging firm John Williams could not have guessed what the future had in

store. But he may well have had high hopes - John Williams had no fewer than ten children, four of them boys.

The eldest son, Fred, took an interest in the business and for some time held the job of store manager. He combined this role with selling paint for Beards but died early in 1948.

John Williams' second son, Harry, was with the CIS for most of his working life, having left the family firm at an early age. However he returned to the fold at the age of 65 upon retirement from the CIS, to take up a directorship which he held until 1966. Harry's son Jack joined

the company after being demobilised from the army in 1946 and stayed with the business until his retirement in 1986.

Horace Williams, the founder's third son, spent all his working life in the engineering side of the business, bringing the technical knowledge he had received serving with the Royal Engineers during the war to bear in the company workshops and service departments.

Lastly, Vincent, the fourth and youngest son, became company secretary, then managing director and finally chairman. He died in 1982 in his 75th year without ever retiring from the firm.

Such a future was far from John William's mind 60 years earlier: the economic boom which had followed the end of the Great War in 1918 was all too quickly coming to an end. Businesses which had been enjoying considerable prosperity now found themselves under immense pressure. Over the coming decade tens of thousands would close. The worst economic depression in modern history lay just around the corner. For those engaged in old fashioned or outdated enterprises the end was certain.

In 1922 the Williams wheelwright business had moved to Trafford Street where it was installed in a series of arches. By 1926 however it was obvious to all but the blind that horse-drawn traffic was in decline: John Williams and his sons wisely decided to transfer to motor maintenance.

The company started a round-the-clock motor vehicle maintenance service, including the use of a converted breakdown vehicle, believed to be the very first to operate in the Manchester area.

The Williams family soon obtained appointments as official repairers to the leading insurance companies, and it was not long before they found the increasing number of customers more than justified their venture in the motor vehicle trade.

Britain in the 1930s was hardly booming however: those on short time were the lucky ones - millions of others were unemployed. Traditional industries were in decline everywhere and if such misery were not enough over on the far side of the North Sea was the spectre of German Nazi militarism, a threat which most folk prayed was only an illusion.

Left: War-time vehicles at Whitworth Street West, Manchester.

Although most industries were in decline and barely treading water, a few survived and often managed to grow.

This was certainly true of the motor industry whose replacement of horses by horsepower was an unstoppable economic imperative. The Williams family had made exactly the right choice at the right time.

Surviving the 1930s was an achievement in itself. But the catalyst for rapid change would be the declaration of war in 1939.

The Williams company carried on trading in a relatively small way until 1940 when it started to function as an army auxiliary workshop in conjunction with the Royal Electrical and Mechanical Engineers who were stationed on the site until the end of the war in 1945.

This type of military work continued after the war: in 1947 the Ministry of Defence offered the firm a central workshop in Fazakerley, Liverpool.

All government work was subsequently transferred from Manchester to Liverpool. The operation at Trafford Street reverted to private, commercial and insurance repair work: gradually over the next decade or so the volume of business increased due to the return of post war private motoring.

In the late 1940s and the 1950s that return however was hardly spectacular, to begin with: petrol rationing and a severe shortage of new cars was hardly the workers' paradise that the electorate had expected when they voted in the country's first Labour Government in 1945.

Not until the late 1950s would the economy recover sufficiently for Prime Minister Harold Macmillan to be able to announce that we had 'never had it so good'.

The Prime Minster was right; we really had never had it so good: full employment was back, rationing was ended and the novelty of the new 'hire purchase' made it possible for folk to buy goods they had once only dreamed of. A dream shared, and now fulfilled, by many was owning a car.

In 1960 the Williams Company opened a car showroom on Deansgate for the purpose of selling new and used cars under the Rootes franchise. In 1970 its current BMW franchise was acquired. By this time the bodyshop side of the business had moved from Trafford Street to new premises on Hadfield Street, from which it continues to operate today.

Parkway at the southern gateway to the city. The imposing building now holds an impressive stock of Land Rovers in a broad range of specifications, colours and models.

In addition, two new dealerships to house BMW Motorcycles and MINI also opened in 2000 and 2001 respectively.

Expansion was now the order of the day. In 2002 the company acquired the Ian Anthony group in Bolton, and in 2003 Howarth BMW and Howarth MINI in Rochdale. The Rochdale operation subsequently moved into a £4m purpose built showroom incorporating the latest in technology breaking the mould in design for car dealerships in the UK.

Yet another branch of the company, known as PSV, was opened in 1973 to convert vans into mini-buses and coaches. Production took place in Liverpool but the sales division was in Manchester. The initial success of this branch was due in no small measure to the introduction of the breathalyser test by Transport Minister Barbara Castle. Fear of prosecution gripped the public, and pubs, clubs and hotels were all arranging their own transport.

Williams had this branch of business to themselves at first. Later, through competition in this sector of the market, Williams' share dropped and the company decided to consolidate production and sales back in Manchester. PSV continued to trade until 1996.

The company built a prestigious purpose-built facility on Upper Brook Street in 1984 to where it transferred the new car sales, service and parts operation whilst continuing to retail used vehicles from its Deansgate showroom.

Some five years later Williams built an additional showroom adjacent to its main site solely for retailing used BMW vehicles. The closure of the Deansgate showroom enabled the company to offer its full range of services on one site.

In 2000 Land Rover was added to the Williams offer when the company built premises just off the Princess

Today the company continues to represent BMW in both the Manchester and Liverpool city centres, and has recently responded to demand by building a state-of-the-art bodyshop facility at Pall Mall in Liverpool adjacent to its Great Howard Street site.

BMW continues to be at the forefront of vehicle design and manufacture. Williams is committed to supporting the franchise by combining the latest in technology with its traditional high quality service to all of its customers. The Williams mission statement is 'Right first time, on time, every time' and working under the strapline 'The difference is Williams' the operation continues to be hugely successful whilst maintaining long-established family values at the heart of the business.

Not bad progress for a firm which set out as Wheelwright's repairing horse-drawn vehicles!

*Left: The premises on Deansgate shortly after completion in 1960. **Above:** An exterior view of the prestigious premises on Upper Brook Street. **Right:** The interior of the 'high tech' new car showroom.*

Manchester Airport - The Sky's the Limit

Today Manchester Airport offers travellers more destinations than any other UK airport, with over 100 airlines flying to more than 215 destinations. Over 22 million passengers fly from Manchester each year.

Older readers will have memories of what was in their younger days still known as Ringway Airport or the now archaic-sounding, Ringway Aerodrome.

A few readers will be old enough to recall Charles Lindbergh's epic solo flight across the Atlantic in 1927, but far fewer will be old enough to recall witnessing the first aeroplanes to fly from Manchester back in the days when aircraft pilots were still grandly known as aviators.

In 1919 Britain's first-ever scheduled air service was launched from the private airfield at Alexandra Park,

connecting Manchester to Southport and Blackpool. Manchester Corporation set up a committee to investigate the feasibility of a new airport and purchased land at Barton near Eccles.

In 1928 members of the Chamber of Commerce had commented 'If those interested in aviation can show that arrangements can be made to secure a Manchester aerodrome without undue addition to the City's rates the Chamber will give its approval and sympathy to their suggestion'. Meanwhile the Corporation built a temporary airfield at Wythenshawe which opened in 1929 making the Manchester the United Kingdom's first municipality to have its own licensed aerodrome.

Above: An early aerial view of Manchester Airport.
Below: Manchester Airport's main passenger terminal circa 1950.

The 1st January 1930 witnessed the opening of a permanent airport at Barton. An aircraft from Northern Air Transport made the inaugural landing: the first scheduled service began on 16th June – Imperial Airways, three times a week on the Croydon-Birmingham-Manchester-Liverpool circuit.

The City Council and KLM, Royal Dutch Airlines, were discussing possible air links, but the Barton site would have needed an expensive runway extension to achieve this. However, Ringway, south of Manchester, had potential and the available land: the Council resolved to build new facilities there – by just 55 votes to 54! In 1935 the building work began and Ringway was officially opened in June 1938. In its first 14 months of operation Ringway handled 7,600 passengers.

Such numbers may not sound large today, but in the days before radar, pressurised cabins, in-flight films, auto-pilots and ultra-low fares these figures were enormous, and demonstrate not only the high local demand for rapid travel, but also the ability of local folk to pay the substantial costs involved.

A golden age of air travel appeared to be about to dawn – only to be cruelly deferred by the rise of Herr Hitler and his invasion of Poland in 1939.

With the declaration of war in September 1939 most aerodromes became RAF bases. Ringway however was never requisitioned during World War II, but it still played a crucial part in the war effort. Fairey and Avro both operated manufacturing and maintenance bases there for thousands of military aircraft, including the construction of such famous wartime types as the Beaufighter, Halifax, Battle, Fulmar, York and Barracuda, plus the development of the all-important Lancaster bomber. Early glider-borne warfare techniques were also developed there, in addition to operations by the SOE (forerunner of today's SAS).

Ringway's most famous role however, was as the centre for the training of Airborne Forces. Over 60,000 paratroopers were trained at Ringway and nearby Tatton Park, including soldiers from Poland, Czechoslovakia, Belgium, France, Holland, Norway, Canada and the USA, making a total of 429,800 jumps.

The war years saw the construction of three tarmac runways, ten new hangers and much additional infrastructure.

In retrospect the war was to prove the greatest possible catalyst to air travel. Advances in technology, such as radar and the jet engine, would transform the aviation industry.

Above: *A busy Pier B, part of Manchester Airport's original Terminal 1 in the mid 1970s.*

An Air France Dakota flying from Paris marked the start of the airport's post-war operations: within seven months of re-opening 10,000 passengers had passed through Ringway.

By 1947 throughput was 34,000 passengers per year, and in 1949 extended terminal facilities opened. The main runway was extended in 1951, and in 1952 a 24-hour operation began: 1952 was also the year that the airport saw its first transatlantic departure —though only as a result of an emergency stopover made by a plane bound for Jamaica. The following year the Belgian airline, Sabena, introduced the first scheduled transatlantic service to New York. In 1954 Ringway Airport was renamed Manchester Airport, and a year later the first package holiday flight took off bound for Ostend.

Not that in the early days of package holidays every destination could be expected to match the standard set in Manchester: those who flew to Mallorca for example would find they not only had to switch to a smaller plane in Spain but on reaching their final destination discover found their new transport landing not at an airport but on the beach!

Since then millions upon millions of satisfied holiday makers have begun their journeys from Manchester Airport, a memorable experience made all the more so by its excellent facilities with an atmosphere which is akin to that which was once encountered in the world's great termini in the days when steam was king.

In 1962 HRH the Duke of Edinburgh opened a new terminal (now part of Terminal 1), the first in Europe to enable passengers to pass totally under cover from the terminal to the plane using the new pier system. In 1974 major redevelopment began including the construction on an additional pier, taking passenger capacity to five million, and in 1978 Manchester was designated the only Gateway International Airport outside London. By this time more than 5,000 people were employed by more than 100 companies operating at the airport.

A runway extension, opened by HRH Princess Anne in 1982 meant Manchester could attract long-haul operators. The World Freight terminal opened in 1986 and Manchester Airport PLC was formed – the shareholders being the ten metropolitan districts of Greater

*Top: The famous lead crystal chandeliers of Terminal 1's main departure concourse. **Above:** A recent ariel view of Terminals 1 and 3.*

Manchester: Manchester City Council owning 55 per cent of the shares, with 5 per cent each being allocated amongst the nine smaller metropolitan districts. By June 1987 Manchester had handled one million passengers in one month for the first time and in 1988 it celebrated its Golden Jubilee. The following year HRH the Princess of Wales opened the Domestic Terminal.

In 1992 proposals for a second runway were published. The Aviation Viewing Park was opened in 1992 and the following year HRH the Duke of Edinburgh opened Terminal 2, doubling capacity to 20 million passengers per year. The same year the airport's own railway station was opened as part of long term plans to enhance public transport to the airport. In 1997 plans for the second runway were approved and work began almost immediately. Integral to the work was a £17 million programme of environmental measures to minimise the impact on the countryside and local communities. Manchester Airport PLC acquired a major shareholding in Humberside Airport in 1999.

On 5th February 2001 the first commercial flight - by Emirates to Dubai – took off from the £172 million Runway 2 – the United Kingdom's first new full-length commercial runway built for 20 years. In April 2001 the Airport Company completed its purchase of East Midlands and Bournemouth airports.

The Prime Minister, the Rt Hon. Tony Blair MP, officially opened the second runway in May 2001. In 2002 Manchester Airport acted as a major sponsor for the highly successful Commonwealth Games. 2003 saw the opening by BMI baby of a major base at the airport, and the airport's busiest ever 24-hour period with 942 aircraft movements as the city hosted the UEFA Champions League final. Also that year the Ground Transport Interchange – The Station – opened. In 2004 Manchester Airport reached the milestone of 20 million passengers per annum. By the end of 2005 Manchester Airport had handled 22.75 million passengers during the year, and more than 150,000 tonnes of freight.

Today more than 19,000 people work at the airport, around 2,000 of whom are employees of Manchester Airport PLC which has responsibility for the buildings, runways, taxiways and land, including car parks. The company also provides the fire and security services.

In 2005, Manchester Airport contributed more than £3.2 billion to the UK economy and over 130,000 jobs nationwide can be attributed to the Airport's operations.

The scale of present activity at Manchester Airport would have been truly inconceivable to Captain AN Kingway the dashing aviator who made the first landing at Wythenshawe on 2nd April 1929 – perhaps almost as inconceivable as it would have been to the inhabitants of the Bronze Age settlement the remains of which were uncovered during excavations for the airport's second runway.

What next for Manchester's multi-award winning airport? Who can say, when the sky is the limit?

Top: *A Singapore Airlines Boeing 747 departs from Manchester Airport.* **Below:** *Checking in for flights at the £60m public transport hub, The Station.*

Bauer Millett & Co - Nothing but the best

When specialist car dealer Bauer Millett & Co Ltd announced in 2006 that it was to move to new premises, those in the know licked their lips in anticipation.

The exotic nature of the cars sold by Bauer Millett attracts entrepreneurs, successful businessmen, company directors and most fundamentally car enthusiasts as keen customers. Equally keen are all we inveterate window shoppers, planning what to do with that long overdue lottery win!

The new and much larger facility based at Lawrence House inside the viaduct arches beneath the G-Mex car park on Albion Street, opposite the Hacienda and Bridgewater Hall, would fulfil their promise to be the most impressive showroom the company has ever had.

Moving into the new premises on Albion Street not only gave the company the ability to display and present its vehicles in better surroundings than ever before, but also more than doubled the size of the company's car sales operation.

Currently Bauer Millett is the sole official UK dealer for Hummer 4x4s, a marque which thanks to film star and celebrity-owners such as Arnold Schwarzenegger, has received vast amounts of media attention over recent years. The company also specialises in American cars as well as exotic European vehicles.

As a result of specialising the company sells cars to customers right across the whole country – and

Above: Founders Chris Bauer and Lawrence Millett.
Below: Lawrence Millett outside the company's Peter Street showroom alongside two 1977 Pontiac Firebird Trans Am's. Made hugely popular by Burt Reynolds in the hit movie 'Smokey and the Bandit' the Firebird was regarded as America's performance car of the 1970s.

established business come into being - and who were Messrs Bauer and Millett?

The company was founded by two partners Chris Bauer and Lawrence Millett. Bauer Millett & Co Ltd was officially incorporated on 12th June 1973.

Both Chris and Lawrence shared a passion for unusual quality cars. As a result the company's main focus has always been the sale of prestige vehicles.

Chris had sold cars from his home before starting his own garage in Blakeley in 1970. Whilst running his garage in Blakeley Chris Bauer had begun buying part-exchange vehicles from Lawrence Millett who then worked at another garage, Sports Motors.

Lawrence started his career in the motor industry at the age of 16 working for Sid Abrams as an apprentice mechanic overhauling gearboxes. After a number of years his enthusiasm convinced Sid to promote him to car sales. He later continued as a salesman at Sports Motors, working for Rodney Bloor where he would meet Chris Bauer.

Chris had been working at Blakeley for three years, before Lawrence joined forces with him in early 1973 to found Bauer Millett & Co Ltd. Soon after they moved premises to the BOC garages in Bolton.

In retrospect 1973 was one of the worst years ever in which to begin a new business dealing in prestige cars. Inflation was soaring, reaching almost 30 per cent a year; VAT had been introduced in the United Kingdom on 1st April by a government struggling to get a grip on a

even supplies the occasional vehicle to long-standing customers overseas.

Though currently an exotic and American car specialist, as well as being an authorised agent for Hummer, at different times during the 1980s the firm has also held official franchises for Volkswagen, Audi, Alfa Romeo and Lancia motorcars. It has also been a franchised dealer for Harley Davidson motorcycles.

Today Bauer Millett is not merely the only exotic/prestige car dealer in Manchester city centre, it is in fact the only city centre car dealership.

It is of course a magnet for anyone with an interest in unusual and prestige cars, but how did this now-long

Top: One of many Rolls Royce stocked by Bauer Millett.
Above: A 1977 Alfa Romeo Alfetta GTV.
Right: A 1976 Morgan Plus 8 V8.

collapsing economy. And worse was to follow: on October 6th Israel attacked Egypt and was itself attacked by Syria on the Golan Heights.

UK Premier Ted Heath announced the launch of Phase Three of his counter inflationary policy just as Israel launched a wave of tanks across the Suez Canal. On 17th October Arab oil producers announced a cut in oil supplies until Israel withdrew from occupied territories. Inevitably petrol prices at the pump escalated dramatically.

And prestige vehicles have a notable tendency to be thirsty beasts. With petrol prices going through the roof 1973 was hardly a good year to begin specialising in the sale of fuel-hungry luxury cars.

Yet quality counts. And customers with a real love of exotic cars, and deep enough pockets, were not going to be put off merely by the inconvenience and expense of high fuel consumption.

From the outset Chris handled the bulk of the car buying whilst Lawrence focussed on the sales side. Success relied on Chris and Lawrence's abilities to buy sought-after vehicles at the right time and at favourable cost, earning themselves a reputation for being able to get cars that others could not.

Chris and Lawrence started off entirely on their own; today the company has over 20 employees – though at the time the company had a Harley Davidson franchise numbers rose as high as 40 staff.

Over the years the company has attracted a number of key employees who have remained with it for decades and have helped make it what it has become. Alan Bowen for example, one of the company's workshop technicians has clocked up more than 30 years; Nigel Ruffley, Sales Director, has been with the company almost as long, whilst Chris McDonald, Workshop Manager, has more than a quarter of a century on the clock.

The business has occupied a number of addresses over the years, starting with the BOC garages in Bolton from 1973 until 1975. From there it moved to Peter Street Manchester opposite the Great Northern Railway building for 20 years, and for a time also occupied a showroom in front of Finglands Bus Depot on Wilmslow Road.

Of particular help in the early days was Joe Sunlight, the acclaimed architect and property developer. Joe had a soft spot for Chris and Lawrence and gave them a favourable start when they opened the showroom on Peter Street in property owned by him.

Top: *The 1977 Chevrolet Corvette, the car picture was sold by the company to London Nightclub owner Peter Stringfellow.* ***Below:*** *The 1973 Ford Mustang Convertible, the only convertible of Ford's entire range on offer to the American public in this year.*

When the company took on a franchise for Harley Davidson motorcycles a new showroom was opened at 325 Deansgate.

From Peter Street the company moved to the former ambulance station at 297 Deansgate and later to 325 Deansgate, shortly after the decision was made to stop selling Harley Davidsons.

Until 1989 Chris Bauer and Lawrence Millett ran the business together; that year however, Lawrence bought out Chris' share in the business so that Chris could pursue other interests in the property market. In 2004 Mitch Millett Lawrence' son joined the business.

Sadly Lawrence Millett passed away in 2005. Today Mitch Millett is carrying on the family business as Managing Director, imbued with exactly the same appreciation for exotic and prestige vehicles as his father.

And it's not just about sales.The company also has the ability to maintain particular American vehicles which cannot be maintained effectively by anyone else in Britain, as well as having the only trained personnel to do so.

With over 20 years of GM franchise experience, Bauer Millett services, repairs and maintains all General Motors

North American vehicles. The Manchester city centre facility has the 'Tech 2' equipment and technology to diagnose and repair all GM products. The company has been the United Kingdom's only official Hummer dealer since 2003, and is the UK's official centre for warranty repairs. Highly trained technicians are also experienced repairers of Dodge, Chrysler and Ford cars or trucks.

Bauer Millett is an official supplier of General Motors Parts for North American Vehicles. From a stock in excess of 30,000 part numbers, highly trained staff identify parts using the latest GM 'Microcat' system. The company can also supply most parts for North American Ford, Lincoln and Dodge vehicles.

Today a glance at Bauer Millett's stock is like entering petrol-head heaven. Names like Cadillac, Ford Mustang, Corvette, Dodge, Mercury, Rolls Royce and Bentley instantly evoke images of strength, status and the last word in luxury.

Back in 1973, when the firm of Bauer Millett & Co Ltd was founded by two men who enjoyed such cars every bit as much as their customers, who could have predicted where it would lead? Indeed, given the world oil crisis of that year, many folk would have predicted nothing but doom and gloom for the fledgling firm.

Happily, now in the 21st century, the doomsayers got it wrong. There is always room at the top – and for car buyers of Manchester and the rest of Britain Bauer Millett & Co still offers nothing but the best.

Top: The Cortina Crayford MK 5 Convertible Coupé launched by Crayford at the 1980 Birmingham NEC Motor Show. Above left: A view inside the Bauer Millett show-room at Peter Street. Below: Bauer Millett's new Lawrence House premises in Albion Street. Below inset: A selection of exotic cars stocked by the company.

Waters MS Technologies Centre / Micromass UK Ltd - Solving the mystery of molecules

How do you test medicines to ensure that they are not counterfeit? How do you test soil, water and food for pollutants, or industrial chemicals for purity?

The magic of mass spectrometry is the answer. And when it comes to mass spectrometry the best magicians in the business are to be found in the North West of England at Micromass UK Ltd., now the Waters MS Technologies Centre, a company based in Floats Road, Wythenshawe.

Mass spectrometry is a means of analysing the tiniest amounts of substances to see what they are made up of at the atomic level. And its no coincidence that Manchester should be at the cutting edge of such applied science.

In 1808 John Dalton a Manchester Quaker schoolmaster and self-educated chemist published his atomic theory in a book, his 'New System of Chemical Philosophy'. The theory was derived from, and rested upon, the observation that elements combine in fixed proportions according to their weights. John Dalton Street in Manchester was named in his honour.

Dalton was the first scientist to use experimental evidence to support the hypothesis that all element are made up of tiny, invisible, indivisible and unalterable atoms, each

exactly the same as all other atoms of the same element, and each of which has a weight which could be calculated as a fixed multiple of the weight of an atom of hydrogen, the lightest element.

Almost a century later another Mancunian showed part of Dalton's picture of atoms to be not quite true. Sir Joseph John Thompson was born in Cheetham Hill, Manchester and educated at Owens College before going to Cambridge in 1876. He subsequently became director of the famous

Above: Robert Craig, founder of VG Micromass in 1968. *Above right:* Alf Monks and Norman Lynaugh standing next to an early mass spectrometer. *Right:* A view of the Micromass 70-70 high resolution mass spectrometer, the first new product developed in Altrincham in 1975.

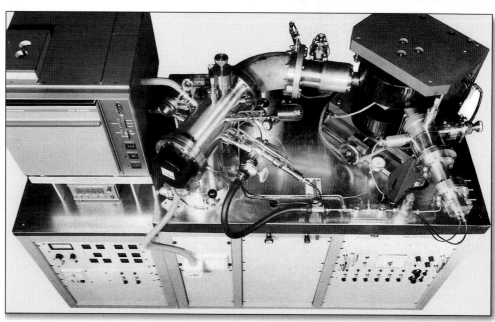

Cavendish Laboratory in 1884. Thompson would claim the honour of being the man who discovered the electron, the first known sub-atomic particle.

In 1904 Thompson built an apparatus which allowed streams of electrically charged atoms and similarly charged molecules (collectively known as ions) to be separated according to their mass. This was in effect the very first mass spectrometer, and in 1912 would famously lead to the discovery of the existence of isotopes – slightly different versions of atoms of the same element. The mass spectrograph subsequently developed by one of Thompson's students in the 1920s, Nobel Prize-winner, Francis Aston, allowed the mass, or weight, of atoms and molecules to be measured. JJ Thompson himself deservedly received the 1906 Nobel Prize for Physics, and a knighthood in 1908. On his death in 1940, on the eve of the Battle of Britain, such was Thompson's fame that he would be buried in Westminster Abbey near the remains of Isaac Newton.

By the time of World War II all the isotopes of naturally occurring elements had been discovered and measured using mass spectrometry.

During the war the research department of Metropolitan Vickers (MV) Electrical Company at Manchester's Trafford Park, a company already experienced in vacuum engineering, built mass spectrometers for the United Kingdom Department of Scientific and Industrial Research as part of the development of the first atomic weapons.

Following the end of the second world war the research department at Metropolitan Vickers continued to manufacture mass spectrometers for use in the analysis and identification of organic and inorganic substances. The earliest instruments made went to universities and petroleum companies.

The team at the MV research department worked, under Robert Craig, on the design and development of high-resolution mass spectrometers. In 1960 Metropolitan Vickers merged with other companies to form Associated Electrical Industries (AEI) and during the next decade became a world leader in the supply of high-resolution mass spectrometers.

In 1968 Robert Craig, foreseeing an unsettled future at AEI following a takeover by GEC, moved to Vacuum Generators (VG) in East Grinstead. Vacuum Generators had been formed in 1962 by B Eastwell and colleagues to manufacture vacuum components. An embryonic mass spectrometer manufacturing programme was launched by Robert Craig and the early instruments were sufficiently successful to encourage the formation of VG Micromass Ltd, which in 1969, with a total of seven staff, moved to Winsford in Cheshire near to Manchester.

In December 1973 VG Micromass was split into several new companies, and two of them, VG Organic and VG Data Systems moved to Broadheath, Altrincham under the

Above: An aerial view of Floats Road, Wythenshawe, factory opened in 1981.

management of Brian Green. The rationale behind the split was B Eastwell's 'Christmas Card Principle' – most people send Christmas cards to 50-100 people, a number which represents a natural maximum of number of people who can really get to know each other in a company and work together as a team.

VG Organic developed its first high-resolution mass spectrometer, the Micromass 70-70, in 1974. The first instrument was delivered to Oxford University in 1975 and was in use until 1997 when it was decommissioned and presented to the Manchester Museum of Technology.

During the 1980s VG Organic and VG Datasystems was further split up to become VG Analytical, VG Masslab, VG Tritech and VG Biotech – each company selling different types of mass spectrometer to different but commonly overlapping markets.

Below: *A group of instruments in development at Floats Road, Wythenshawe, in 1985. The picture shows Peter Bott, now the Projects Program Manager, in the foreground working on a ZAB-4F - a tandem magnetic sector mass spectrometer and at the time the world's largest commercial mass spectrometer.* ***Right:*** *Brian Green being congratulated by Barry Mulady, then Managing Director of VG Analytical, for being awarded the OBE in 1985. Other Directors of the company are standing in the background, including Alf Monks and Norman Lynaugh (far right).*

In that same decade Brian Green who managed VG Organic when it was first established in Altrincham back in 1973 was awarded the OBE in recognition of his contribution to mass spectrometry technology.

In 1986 the company won the Queen' Award for Exports and the following year the Queen's Award for Technology.

In 1991 the VG Group of Companies, by now owned by British American Tobacco (BAT) was sold to Fisons plc. Four years later in 1995 Fisons, the then troubled pharmaceutical company, decided to divest itself of its scientific instrument businesses. As a consequence the Manchester-based mass spectrometry companies (VG Analytical, VG BioTech and VG IsoTech) were acquired in 1996 by a management team led by Norman Lynaugh to become the newly constituted Micromass (UK) Ltd.

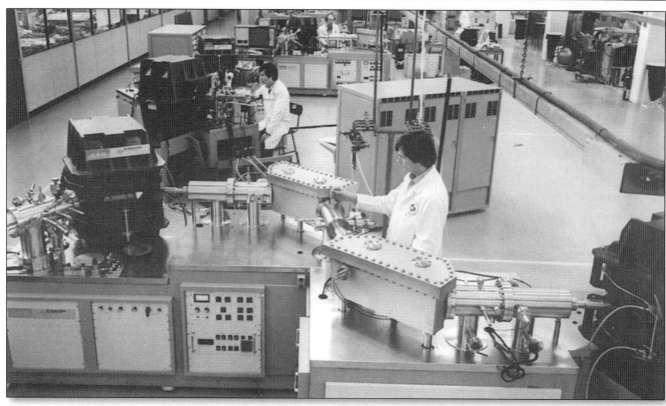

mass spectrometer that allows detection and identification of less than a pico-gram of a substance. A pico-gram is a millionth of a millionth of a gram, not only too small to be seen with the naked eye but almost too small even to imagine.

In 2006 Waters introduced a new instrument that not only allows the mass of molecules to be measured but also their shape and size. This instrument, developed by Micromass in Manchester, is the world's first commercial mass spectrometer to provide this capability.

At the outset Micromass employed some 250 people at its two sites: Broadheath, Altrincham and Floats Road Wythenshawe. By 2001 the number of employees in Manchester had swollen to 350 and Micromass opened a third site at Atlas Park, Simonsway, Wythenshawe. Today Micromass employs more than 400 people in the Manchester area.

In 1997 the Waters Corporation, a US-based company with headquarters in Milford near Boston, Massachusetts, acquired Micromass.

Since 1958, Waters Corporation has been in the business of making analytical instruments that assist scientists in reaching their scientific goals. Whether at work discovering new pharmaceuticals, inventing new and more effective ways to treat diseases, assuring the safety of the world's food and drinking water supplies, monitoring and controlling pollution, or conserving the world's greatest art treasures, scientists worldwide rely on Waters liquid chromatography and mass spectrometry products.

Approaching nearly 50 years in business, Waters is now one of largest companies in the analytical instruments industry, supporting scientists working in the world's 100,000 laboratories.

Waters Corporation is a world leader in the supply of liquid chromatography equipment. Liquid chromatography and mass spectrometry compliment each other perfectly: a complex mixture may first be separated into its constituent parts and each component may be analysed and identified by the mass spectrometer as it 'elutes' or leaches out from the chromatograph.

In 2000 Micromass won two Queen's Awards, one for International Trade and one for Innovation. These awards were a consequence of the development of the Q-TOF mass spectrometer, a novel tandem quadrupole 'time-of-flight'

Micromass is now primarily engaged in the business of developing and researching novel and leading edge mass spectrometry instrumentation. The company is also engaged in the design, engineering and manufacturing of mass spectrometers for distribution through the Waters distribution network. The instruments are sold throughout the world to universities, government research institutes, contract laboratories and to industry. They are used primarily in the analysis of chemicals and biochemicals and have applications in the chemical, pharmaceutical, biotechnology and petroleum industries, in the life sciences and in environmental monitoring.

Two hundred years on since John Dalton developed his atomic theory it's thanks to firms like Micromass that the words 'science' and Manchester still remain inextricably linked.

Top: A view of instruments at various stages of assembly in the workshop at Floats road, Wythenshawe, 1985.
Below: Bob Bordoli, then Managing Director of VG Analytical, receiving the Queen's Award in 1987 from the Lord Lieutenant of Manchester, employees raise a glass in the background.

Desser & Co - Never sparing the cane!

A conservatory somehow isn't really complete without some cane furniture. Throughout the United Kingdom and Eire hundreds of garden centres and other outlets supply thousands of customers with stylish lightweight chairs tables and other fine examples of the basket weaver's art. But from where do those outlets get their supplies? The answer, surprisingly enough, is likely to be Manchester and the firm of Desser and Company Ltd, a business which has been specialising in importing and distributing such items since the end of the first world war.

Desser and Company Limited, Britain's leading importer and distributor of cane furniture and wickerware has a proud heritage stretching back over four generations of the same family.

Above: Founder Issac Desser.
Right: Simon Desser, brother of the founder.
Below: The company's warehouse in Lyon Street, 1930s.

The fascinating story starts in the dark days of the Great War when Isaac Desser, then a young soldier in the British Army, was posted to serve on the front line in Belgium. It was there that for the first time he came into contact with Flemish craftsmen who were producing various types of basketware – and an idea was born.

Realising the commercial potential of what he had seen, on his return home on being demobbed from the army Isaac quickly set to work on putting into action his plan to import baskets from Belgium for sale in Britain.

Like many new family businesses Desser & Co had humble beginnings. At first it was run from the front parlour of Isaac's Mother-in-law's terraced house in Whitfield Street,

Manchester, where his wife Annie and her family helped pack the goods for despatch to customers.

When the family moved to a new house in nearby Cheetham Hill Road the business went with them. Isaac was soon joined by his brother Simon, and in 1919 Desser and Company was formed.

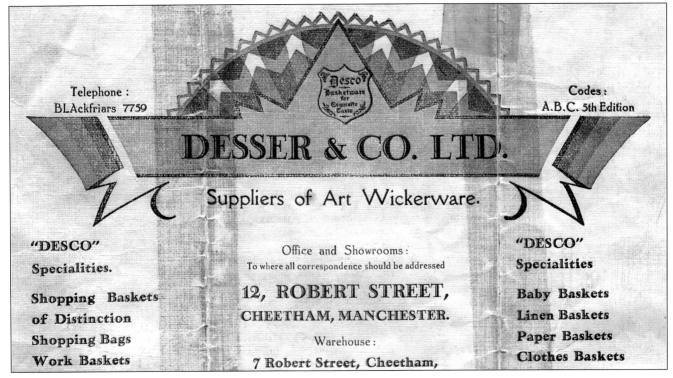

During the 1920s the business continued to expand, necessitating a move to a larger, but still cramped, basement in Robert Street.

In 1932 Isaac's son Morris joined the company – at the same time as a young secretary Miriam Marcus. Romance soon blossomed and she became Mrs Miriam Desser, continuing to make a contribution to the company over many years.

Despite the Depression of the 1930s Isaac, Simon and Morris continued to expand the business, and this necessitated a third move, this time to a warehouse in Lyon Street, still within the Cheetham Hill area.

After the second world war Simon's Son-in-law Ronnie Stewart joined the company which was now housed in Lord Street, Cheetham. Sadly Simon Desser died shortly after the move.

The company continued to grow in the post war years, importing wickerware from all across Europe, from behind the Iron Curtain, and eventually even from the Peoples Republic of China.

This meant that Morris Desser had to make buying trips away from home for long periods to Eastern Europe, Asia and to countries which were not always hospitable or comfortable.

By now Morris' son Gordon had joined the business, followed by Ronnie's two sons Michael and Barry.

Further expansion signalled another move in the early 1970s to an impressive purpose-built warehouse and showroom in Bradstone Road, Cheetham where the company is still based today.

A cane suite bought from or through Desser has been individually made by hand using the highest quality materials to the most exacting standards of design and finish. If properly cared for it will provide a lifetime of use and pleasure.

But what exactly is cane, and where does it come from?

Sometimes confused with bamboo, canes can usually be distinguished because they are solid; by contrast bamboos are almost always hollow. The annual international trade in rattans and canes is worth several billion pounds.

This page: Early Desser & Co Limited letterheads.

In the 1970s Indonesia became the world's major supplier of rattan, accounting for nearly 70 percent of the entire global trade. Since then, the trade profile had undergone dramatic changes.

Trade in rattan has burgeoned into a multimillion-dollar industry. Trade in raw rattan worldwide was in the order of $50 million. By the time the finished product reaches the consumer, its value has increased to $1.2 billion. Overall, the global trade is worth $4 billion.

The value of export increased a stupendous 250-fold in just 17 years in Indonesia. The rise has been 75-fold in 15 years in the Philippines, 23-fold in 9 years in Thailand and 12-fold in 8 years in Malaysia. Indonesia, the market leader, has now set its target for exports at $700 million, while Singapore aims at a target of $60 million.

Rattans are climbing palms that provide the raw material for the cane-furniture industry. Although there are some climbing palms in the Americas, the true rattans are restricted to the tropics and subtropics of the Old World.

The plants are particularly abundant in South-east Asia, especially in the Malay Archipelago. More than 600 different species have been identified. Their major habitat is tropical rain forest, where in much of South-east Asia they are the most important forest product after timber.

Rattans have long, flexible stems. In optimum growing conditions some species will grow to very great lengths. The longest ever recorded grew to over 175 metres. Some species are single-stemmed while others are multi-stemmed: single-stemmed species provide a single harvest while the multi-stemmed species can be harvested on a sustainable basis.

Rattan gatherers need to pull the canes down from the forest canopy and remove the spiny sheaths, leaves and whips. This leaves the bare cane.

Locally rattans are used for a very wide range of purposes, the most important being in the manufacture of baskets and mats. Undoubtedly rattan remains the most important source of material for making baskets and mats in the South-east Asian region.

Most of the commercially harvested cane was exported to manufacturers in Singapore, Hong Kong, Japan, Europe and North America. Today local manufacture is on the increase.

Until recent decades almost all the rattan that entered world trade was collected from the wild from tropical rain

Top: A 1960s Trade Show.
Above: Morris Desser buying in China.

forests. With forest destruction and conversion, the habitat of rattans decreased rapidly and there was a very real shortage of supply. In the mid 1970s however, forest departments in South-east Asia became increasingly conscious of the vulnerability of rattan supply and began investigations aimed at safeguarding the long-term supply of canes for industry.

Commercial estates of rattan were established in Sabah, East Malaysia during the late 1970s. Commercial rattan planting is however still a risky business venture as there is still much to learn about growing the plants. However, growth rates in the new estates have been amazing - small diameter Calamus trachycoleus and the best large diameter cane Calamus manan have both been recorded as growing 6 metres or more a year.

But apart from profit there are also some unexpected benefits from rattan planting.

Rattan 'hugs' trees and saves them from the loggers axe by providing equal or greater economic benefit than harvesting the timber from the companion tree without disturbing the natural habitat.

Ecologically rattan is very important. It grows in degraded forests and in marginal soil. It can also be introduced artificially in natural forest without disturbing the existing structure and balance.

Rattan can grow in areas which cannot support other produce, for example on land which remains under floodwaters for long periods of time.

However the real beauty as far as conservation is concerned is that rattan can only grow amongst existing trees such as fruit orchards and rubber estates, so its cultivation can accurately claim to encourage forest preservation.

Meanwhile, back in Manchester, company founder Isaac Desser died in 1975 having continued to work almost to his 80th year. His great grandson, Gordon's son Simon, joined Dessers in 1987 becoming the first representative of the fourth generation of the family to work in the business. In 1997 Michael's son Mark also joined the company.

Sadness was again to descend on the company in April 1997 with the death of Morris Desser, and then Ronnie Stewart in 2000.

But though individuals may pass the company continues. Today the present generation of the family is carrying on the business in exactly the same spirit as their predecessors, finding the best products at the best possible price, to the satisfaction of suppliers, wholesale customers and most importantly the ultimate purchaser. And more, they are engaged in a trade which now not only adds to the elegant look of thousands of homes but also promotes the well being of people in faraway countries whilst also helping maintain the environment.

Above left: Morris Desser and Ronnie Stewart pictured in the early 1990s. Left: The company's current premises, pictured in 1975. Top: Part of the Desser & Co fleet.

Wing Yip - A taste of the Orient

In the Ancoats area of Manchester stands an impressive Oriental superstore with a large Chinese pagoda at one corner. The pagoda on the Oldham Road has become a local landmark: it stands as a testament to the man and his family behind the Wing Yip Chinese grocery empire.

In 1959 Mr Wing Yip arrived from Hong Kong with just £10 in his pocket.

Chinese restaurants and Chinese food were virtually unknown outside the Chinatowns in Britain, though a few catered for the small Chinese communities in major cities. There were of course some Britons who were familiar with the delights of the Orient: thousands of British servicemen and women as well as diplomatic staff, administrators and businessmen, had lived in outposts of the former British Empire such as Hong Kong and long remembered the taste of Chinese cuisine.

For most however, Chinese food was completely unknown. Take-away meant either fish and chips or pie and peas. Anyone who had predicted in the late 1950s that within a few decades every High Street would boast a Chinese restaurant or take-away would have been laughed at.

The Chinese ate hundred-year old eggs and bird's nest soup didn't they? And didn't they have rice with everything instead of chips?

And then there were chop-sticks. Why didn't the Chinese eat with a knife and fork?

The British were soon to discover the answers to all these questions and begin their love affair with Chinese food. That love affair has transformed our high streets and our diets.

Wing Yip and his family are descended from the ancient Hakka family. The Hakka people come from the centre of China where its civilisation began.

Arriving in Britain in 1959 Wing Yip went to Liverpool where the Liverpool Hakka Association found him a job washing up in a Chinese restaurant. He was quickly promoted to waiter because he could speak English.

Two years later Wing and two partners opened their own restaurant in a former tea shop in Clacton-on-Sea, Essex which they bought for £500. Fortune smiled on

Above left: Founder, Wing Yip.
Below: The original Wing Yip store in Faulkner Street.
Right: Sammy, Yap and Wing in store the 1970s.

them as a Butlins Holiday Camp operated just outside Clacton in 1962. The restaurants in the camp served their last meal by 9.30pm . Wing and his partners would remain open until midnight providing hungry holiday-makers with their unusual Chinese dishes.

With up to 8,000 holidaymakers and some 2,000 Butlins staff at the height of the summer season, the restaurant owners found they had a thriving business.

The Clacton Chinese restaurant was soon followed by two others, and a take-away in East Anglia. The second restaurant was located in Ipswich quite near to the American air base. The American servicemen and women were already familiar with Chinese food and the restaurant became very popular.

By the late 1960s Wing was looking for new opportuni-ties. Rather than being a restauranteur he thought instead he might do better supplying the many new Chinese restaurants which were now springing up.

Wing had been followed to the UK by his brother Sammy, ten years later, who until then had worked at

the Hilton Hotel in Hong Kong. In 1970 Wing and Sammy opened their first specialist Chinese grocery story in Birmingham. The store stocked more than 1,000 different products, sold initially to local Chinese families for cooking traditional dishes at home as well as to chefs and caterers in restaurants and take-aways.

In those early days the business experienced problems with the UK Customs and port health authorities. Officials did not always know what the Oriental foodstuffs were.

In 1975 the business moved to a large store, and in 1992 the Wing Yip Centre and headquarters in Birmingham was completed.

Earlier Wing and Sammy were joined by a third brother, Lee Sing Yap, who had owned a store in Jamaica.

Wing, Sammy and Lee recognised a need for an Oriental grocery store in the North West. Both Manchester and Liverpool had established Chinese communities who required supplies of quality produce from the Far East.

In 1977 the first Wing Yip store in Manchester opened in Faulkner Street in the heart of the Chinese quarter. This was, and continues to be, run and managed by Lee Sing Yap. When the business outgrew those premises, Wing Yip relocated to Addington Street before moving to Oldham Road.

Wing Yip commissioned a custom-built Chinese superstore to be built on the site in Oldham Road which opened for business in 1985. Continued success led to the redevelopment of the site in 2002 into a Chinese superstore and mini-Chinatown, bringing it in line with the branches in Birmingham and Croydon. Wing Yip's Cricklewood store is currently undergoing a similar multi-million pound redevelopment.

Amongst the businesses included in the Wing Yip Centre in Manchester is the 500 seat Glamorous Restaurant: the décor and style of cuisine offered is that of a typical Hong Kong restaurant.

Wing Yip Manchester also includes an HSBC bank, a hairdresser, accountants, Chinese health care and a porcelain exhibition area.

The company currently supplies the majority of the UK's Chinese restaurants and take-aways as well as non-Chinese outlets and food enthusiasts who like to recreate authentic dishes. Wing Yip provides a one stop centre, with secure, well-lit, car parking - customers will travel up to 50 miles to shop.

The Wing Yip own-brand sauce range is well known by Chinese and non-Chinese chefs. The consumer sauce range was launched in 1999 and can be found in high street supermarkets and convenience stores. Flavours include black bean, sweet & sour, spicy Szechuan and Chinese curry.

In 2004 Wing Yip launched an on-line shopping service which, along with more than 900 products, also features easy to follow Oriental recipes and Chinese cultural information.

Each store stocks over 2,500 items, ranging from cooking utensils to unusual products such as chicken's feet.

Every Wing Yip outlet prides itself on personal service. Help to pack bags and load trolleys or cars is standard.

Below: *The custom built Chinese superstore in Oldham Road which opened for business in 1985.*

Beijing under the auspices of the Wing Yip China Fellowship at Churchill College. All staff members, whatever nationality, whose children are at university receive financial assistance from the Trust during their university years.

Yet Wing Yip remains a modest man in the best Confucian tradition. He is not mentioned in Who's Who; he does not play an active role in the business community, nor make large donations to political parties.

The next generation of sons and nephews are already working in the business. Henry Yap is a qualified solicitor and managing director of W Wing Yip & Brothers Property and Investments Ltd. Albert Yip is a qualified pharmacist as well as possessing a degree in business management; he is a Director of the London stores with responsibility for purchasing. Brian Yip holds a degree in banking and finance and is a fully qualified chartered accountant and is responsible for W Wing Yip (International Trading) Ltd. Ennevor Yap has a business management degree and is assistant manager in Manchester. David Yip holds a degree in computer sciences and works in the Manchester store.

The operating business is separate from the family's investments. W Wing Yip & Brothers Trading Group which controls the stores is managed separately from the W Wing Yip Brothers & Property and Investments which oversees the family's property portfolio. Wing Yip himself however remains as chairman: his brothers are also directors of both companies.

Wing and his brothers have also set up the W Wing Yip & Brothers Charitable Trust. The Trust has helped Chinese schools and made donations to the many Chinese Associations throughout the UK. The Trust also donates funds to The Prince's Trust.

The family has also set up the W Wing Yip & Brothers Bursaries to sponsor 30-35 Chinese university students each year, as well as two Chinese students to study at Churchill College Cambridge and one English student to study in China. The company also supports a visiting professor from

According to Wing Yip there is an old Chinese saying – 'Never ask a hero where he comes from.' In England there is another saying: 'Don't judge a man by his words, but by his deeds.'

By anyone's standards, Wing Yip's deeds have ensured him a place among the most prominent and respected members of the UK's Chinese community.

Now the company intends to open even more Wing Yip superstores. As for that £10 which Wing Yip had in his pocket in 1959, today the business has an annual turnover of £80m, and Wing Yip is the only Chinese person in the UK's top 1,000 rich list!

Above and below: *Before and after pictures of the development in Ancoats of the impressive Wing Yip Superstore complete with Pagoda.*
Below Inset: *Sammy, Wing and Yap,2006.*

Salford Van Hire -
Vehicle Hire pioneers for over 40 years

Vehicle hire is not a new concept: readers whose memories stretch back beyond the second world war may recall that it was perfectly possible to visit livery stables in and around Manchester and hire a horse and cart by the hour or for the day in exchange for a few shillings.

Today however things are rather more sophisticated: most people have learned how to drive a motor vehicle, and if the need arises they expect to be able to hire a self-drive van easily and cheaply.

Over the last four decades there has been a quiet revolution in the way people look at vehicle hire. Back then it was usual to hire a 'van and a man'. These days self-drive hire is seen as the simpler and cheaper way forward.

This change is evident more than any other in the North West and one man and one company have been responsible for this change. The man is Raffaello Bacci: the company Salford Van Hire.

Salford Van Hire was founded in 1965 and became a limited company in 1966. It was originally based in Camp Street, Salford, but after five years the need to expand saw it relocating to Sherborne Street, just behind Manchester's Strangeways jail.

Above: *Founder Raffaello Bacci.* **Right:** *The beginning of what has become Britain's largest and most successful privately owned commercial vehicle hire business, 1965.* **Below:** *Part of the growing fleet in the 1970s.*

Above: The company premises in the 1970s.

'SVH' was founded by Raffaello Bacci who came to the United Kingdom in 1951 as a 13-year-old schoolboy to stay with his grandfather Felice Bacci. Raffaello ended up staying in Salford and attending St Boniface's School, just a stone's throw from Camp Street, where his business empire would later be founded. After leaving school Raffaello worked for his grandfather's statuette and lampshade-making business. It was while working for his grandfather that Raffaello realised how difficult it was to hire a van for a short period of time. So he took the decision to buy a van, and to hire it out when he and his grandfather were not using it.

One van soon became two. By the end of the first year in the rental market Raffaello had 12 vans in his fleet. It was the 1960s and business was good. At the end of the second year the fleet had doubled in size, by the third year there were fifty vehicles, and more than a hundred by the end of the fourth year of business.

Part of the success of the business was that its founder insisted on ensuring that the fleet always comprised very new vehicles, maintenance costs were thus kept to a minimum since most were still under manufacturer's warranty. Equally importantly, and a first in the industry, was that Raffaello introduced unlimited mileage vehicle hire, something which made him immensely popular with his customers: vehicle hire was a fixed price for 24 hours with no hidden extras.

The business expanded over the following decades to become the success story it is today. By the mid-1970s there were more than 400 vehicles in the fleet and the world was beginning to sit up and take notice of the business. Today it can boast of having 165 employees, an annual turnover of £48 million, and a fleet of 6,500 vehicles used for commercial and private hire, ranging from small vans to 44 tonne articulated lorries, which are now a regular site on today's busy motorways.

Though he has never fussed too much about appearances Raffaello did buy himself his first Rolls Royce in 1974. It was however an investment: back then you could buy a Rolls and sell it later for the same price it had cost. He bought his for £14,000 and sold it again two years later for the same price.

In 1975, after arriving at Sherborne Street, SVH created a nearby depot especially for car hire, and in the early 1980s took on another nearby site for its contract hire vehicles.

Despite the passage of time Mr. Bacci is still proud to maintain his links with his country of birth. That link has not gone unreciprocated. A full two years before he set up a successful branch of SVH in Tuscany, taking his unique business system back home, the Italian government decided he should be formally recognised, awarding him an Order of Merit in 1986 – the Italian equivalent of an MBE.

Mr. Bacci has been helped by all three of his children, who all still work for the company, keeping it independent and close to its customers in this age of faceless multinational corporate companies. His daughter Graziella started helping out around the company in 1974 as a 12-year-old during her school holidays. From her early days with SVH she also worked in the company's vehicle administration, insurance and general administration departments and had a stint on reception. After studying for a degree in Italian Studies at Manchester University she returned to the company to help her father run the firm.

Graziella's brother Alessandro, born in 1977, also used to help out in his school holidays and also gained an Italian Studies degree at Manchester University before returning to help his family run SVH.

His other daughter, Patrizia born in 1966, helped out at SVH from the age

Right: *Salford Van Hire's service team, 1990.*
Below: *One of the company's freezer fleet vehicles.*

of 15 before obtaining an English Studies degree at Leeds University. Since 1989, she has been based in Italy, running Program Autonoleggio, the Italian arm of SVH's car and van hire operation there.

Despite experiencing several economic recessions during its existence, SVH has been able to come through them all, with the Bacci family viewing such challenges as a way of keeping the company on its toes. Its markets have changed over the years to reflect the major changes that British industry has undergone since the 1960s. In the early days, SVH's main market was in providing vehicles for manufacturers wanting to transport their goods around. This was the main part of the company's business until the late 1970s, by which time a lot of manufacturing had disappeared. In the early 1980s, SVH started to move into

contract hire of vehicles, as more companies looked for the long-term hire of vehicles. By the late 1990s, many major manufacturers and retail companies were handing over their transport responsibilities to firms specialising in it - known as third-party logistics - and this provided another profitable outlet for SVH to develop, as third party logistics companies look to SVH for long-term vehicle hire. The opening decade of the 21st century has seen the company increasing its rental of tractor units and introduced trailers to the fleet to meet increased demand in this sector.

Having been run since its beginnings on the principles of reliability and simplicity, SVH became one of the North West's most famous names. Its distinctive orange, white and black livery is known to millions and there are few people in Greater Manchester who have not either hired or had the benefit of one of their vehicles.

Many thousands of SVH vehicles are now used by companies that are household names - everyone from famous airlines and sweet manufacturers to some of the biggest names in British industry have beaten a path to SVH's door to do business. Many SVH vehicles on long-term hire are painted in the colours of the company that has hired them, so they may not always be recognisable as belonging to Salford Van Hire.

Mr. Bacci's principles of reliability and simplicity have seen the company grow into one of the region's biggest success stories. The company's own livery has remained virtually unchanged since the early years, although the company itself has always kept abreast of changes, and Mr. Bacci likes things to remain as simple and

straightforward as possible. Many of the company's records are still paper-based, as they were in the early days, and SVH believes that keeping things simple helps both the customer and the business.

Meanwhile SVH's ambitions for the future include maintaining the steady expansion it has already enjoyed and keeping delivering the high levels of service that have ensured customers keep coming back time and time again.

Four decades is a long time in business. The changes in Britain over those years have been remarkable. Few businesses founded in 1965 still survive, fewer still have prospered in the way that Salford Van Hire has done. Raffaello Bacci has proved himself beyond doubt to be an exceptional businessman.

Above: A montage of Salford Van Hire vehicles, including recovery and maintenance service's.
Below: Raffaello Bacci and son Alessandro with a small part of the company's 2,500-strong fleet of vans.

Arthur Gresty - A family funeral service

Robert, Margaret and David Gresty are the current directors of the Arthur Gresty family funeral service. The business is run from its main site at Manchester Road, Altrincham, with three satellite branches at Sale Moor, Northenden and Wilmslow.

The company is extremely proud of its standards of service. The current fleet of cars includes two Rolls Royce hearses as well as Mercedes and Rolls Royce limousines. But the most important element of service is personal attention: a standard set in the 1940s.

Company founder, Arthur Gresty, was born in 1908 in Moor Nook, Sale. As a young man he worked as a motor mechanic. Around 1933 however Arthur began working for himself after becoming unemployed.

Arthur married Ethel Gardner from Sale Moor Village in 1934. They had three children: Joan, Elsie and Robert.

Working from his home at 33 Wythenshawe Road, Sale Moor, Arthur built himself a garage for his vehicle maintenance and car hire business. His first car was a 'Bull Nose' Morris Oxford, which he bought for £35 and used as a taxi service specialising in trips to the coast. He eventually swapped his Oxford for a Morris Saloon, which he later exchanged for an Austin Limousine at a cost of £280 (compared to over £68,000 for a limousine today).

Arthur attempted to sign up for wartime service but to his surprise was exempted due to his job. He enrolled in the Home Guard and spent many hours patrolling South Manchester and around Sale Moor.

In 1942, after working over a number of years for local funeral directors, hiring out vehicles and helping with

Above: Founder, Arthur Gresty. Below: Arthur Gresty's first car, a 'Bull Nose' Morris Oxford.

Over the years, the company cars have been used extensively for weddings and high-class chauffer hire. Its vehicles have appeared in a number of TV programmes, such as Coronation Street, and have carried many show business personalities and prominent politicians, not least Margaret Thatcher, Harold Wilson, Edward Heath and Jim Callaghan. They have also been used by members of the Royal family including The Duke of Edinburgh, Princess Margaret, The Duchess of Kent, and the Duke and Duchess of Gloucester: they have also been part of the Royal Cortege on several occasions, when The Queen, Prince Charles and Princess Anne have visited Manchester.

In 1947 Arthur was proud to be accepted into the Pax Vera Masonic Lodge based in Sale. He was a dedicated member of the lodge for 41 years until his death in 1988.

Robert Gresty was born in 1940, the youngest of three children. After studying at Sale Grammar School, in 1956 Robert left to work in partnership with his father in the vehicle side of the business.

During the 1950s planning permission was obtained from Sale Borough Council to use a room at the Sale Moor premises as the first approved private Rest Room covering Sale and Altrincham.

This rest room, whilst being the best around, was not ideal, and the firm tried hard to find better facilities, making several planning applications to Altrincham Borough Council. Every application was rejected. Labour Councillors stated that rest rooms facilities should not be in the hands of private companies and should be 'municipalised'. The Council built a barren, windowless, unplastered room at Hale Cemetery as a supposed rest room. It was never used and is now a storeroom for gardening equipment.

funeral duties, Arthur started his own funeral service. He qualified as a member of the British Institute of Embalmers in 1946, becoming the first qualified embalmer in the locality. He bought an Austin 20 hearse, the first motor hearse to be owned by a Sale funeral director. Later he changed his Austin limousine for a Rolls Royce limousine, another first in the area.

Since then the company has always owned Rolls Royce vehicles, supported at times by Daimler/Mercedes limousines.

In 1945, Arthur leased 'The Garage' at 2a Marsland Road, Sale Moor as a combined garage and funeral directors premises. The following year, he purchased the property.

Top: A day out and a slight delay for Arthur and company.
Above: The company's Sale Moor premises.
Right: A letter from the Pax Vera Lodge inviting Arthur Gresty to attend the Sale Masonic Hall for the purpose of interview by the Lodge Committee

When the Council made the suggestion that the only site they felt suitable as a private rest room was the disused Council slaughterhouse near the gas works, the Gresty family fought back.

The company bought a shop in Ridgeway Road, Timperley and renovated it for rest room use. The Council served an 'enforcement' notice to prevent it from being used. The company however successfully appealed, creating a legal precedent for funeral directors. On appealing for costs, the Minister ruled that the Council had acted irresponsibly.

In 1962 Robert Gresty obtained the Diploma in Funeral Directing, becoming the first qualified Funeral Director in the Sale/Altrincham area. He qualified as an embalmer in the 1970s.

In 1960, the family moved from Sale Moor to Thorley Lane in Timperley. In 1963, after the death of Robert's mother, Robert and his father moved to the current family home at Manchester Road, Altrincham. Robert mainly operated the garage repair centre, petrol sales, MOT centre and chauffer-hire side of the business from the Sale Moor Garage, whilst Arthur built up the Funeral Service.

The business became a limited company in 1965

Robert married his wife, Margaret, a midwife, in 1971 and had two children, David and Helen. Margaret eventually became Robert's co-director, receiving her father-in-law's shares in the company.

Robert Gresty has been National Representative for the Pennine Region of the British Institute of Funeral Directors and past Chairman of the North West Division of the British Institute of Embalmers. He is currently regional Secretary of the BIFD and National Representative for the North West Division of the British Institute of Embalmers.

In the 1970s corporate garages and petrol suppliers flooded the market, buying-out or undercutting small privately-run garages. Robert and Arthur could see the life of their garage was limited and decided to put all their energy into the funeral business.

The garage work was closed down, but the garage was retained to store and maintain the company vehicles. The

Top: Altrincham Crematorium in the 1960s.
Below: A 1960s staff photograph.

The building was transformed into a self-contained funeral home with rest room, mortuary, function room, garaging and parking facilities.

The company has always tried to be at the forefront of modern thinking. In 1981, the company became one of the first Funeral Services in the country to own a computer. Robert had to study, adapt and interlink several software programs to suit the purpose. Robert has since been able to assist a software house writing a specialised system for funeral directors.

Arthur Gresty died in 1988. As a tribute to him, his grandson David opened a new funeral home in Sale Moor in 2005, next door to the garage on Marsland Road, still owned by Robert Gresty.

David Gresty, was born in 1972. Following his A-Levels, he studied engineering and business studies at Bolton Technical College and Salford University, obtaining a Bachelor of Engineering Degree in 1995. He qualified for Membership of the British Institute of Embalmers in 1999 and obtained the Diploma in Funeral Directing for Membership of The British Institute of Funeral Directors in 2006.

David is a past Chairman of the North West Division of The British Institute of Embalmers and became Secretary and Social Secretary in 2005. He married Clare in 2003 and lives in Sale.

Today the Gresty family looks forward to the future with confidence, whilst looking back to the past with understandable pride.

Top left: Outside the company's 2006 funeral home pictured in the 1960s. **Above left:** *Late 1960s Rolls Royce hearses.* **Below:** *A 1970s Rolls Royce shadow later converted into a hearse.*

car hire, taxi work and wedding hire have also been overtaken by the funeral side of the business.

During the last three decades, the company has specialised entirely in providing a comprehensive funeral service. Eight phone lines are staffed 24 hours a day, 7 days a week, 365 days of the year. The company currently has four funeral directors, two full time funeral operatives and a number of other staff to meet clients' needs.

Over the course of those years the company purchased premises in Hall Road, Wilmslow; Ashley Road, Altrincham; Washway Road, Sale and Church Road, Northenden. In 1992 property at Manchester Road, Altrincham was acquired, and in 2005 in Marsland Road, Sale Moor.

During 1982 the Ashley Road premises were extensively rebuilt to appear like a home with an adjacent garage, rather than as a shop. The following year the company rebuilt the front of its Washway Road premises. Both these premises were later sold to make way for the company's most successful funeral home.

This 1930s West Timperley property was originally a private residence until 1990 when it was converted into a hotel. Arthur Gresty Ltd. purchased the property in 1992.

The Manchester Grammar School - Daring pupils to be wise

It is not every school that can claim a history stretching back almost 500 years. The Manchester Grammar School however is a member of an exclusive club whose story reaches back to the 16th century.

It was in 1516 that the Bishop of Exeter, Hugh Oldham, a Lancastrian by birth, paid five pounds to buy a piece of land near the River Irk on which to build a school. By August 1518 when the School opened its doors at Long Millgate the total cost of building had come to 218 pounds 13 shillings and fivepence.

Not content however with simply paying for the building Hugh Oldham also endowed the School with land by the river, and the profits from water driven corn mills. Making the School legally Lord of the Manor, with the power to require its tenants to use its mills, ensured future income. The School's first master was William Plessington who was paid £10 a year.

Boys could be admitted to the School from any part of the country provided they suffered from no contagious disease such as 'pox, leprosy, or pestilence'. The School rules were strict, reflecting the concerns of the times: boys were not allowed to carry knives or staves, nor to indulge in cock fighting or jousting. Astonishing to the present generation of pupils, lessons at the new school began at six in the morning in summer and seven in the winter!

By 1770 the number of boys had increased from 100 to around 150. An additional building had been brought into use in 1776 but by 1808 the growth of Manchester had led to an unhappy change in the School's environs. The site had become surrounded by old buildings chiefly occupied by 'poor people in situations neither healthy nor

Top left: *Long Millgate pictured in the late 1800s. The 1880 Grammar School building can be seen at the end of the street.*
Below: *The gymnasium pictured in the early 1900s.*

comfortable'. Additionally Long Millgate was the venue for the thrice weekly Apple Market.

The road was frequently crowded with horses and carts making it difficult for pupils to make their way from the School to the masters' houses where they boarded. Temptation abounded with older boys resorting to the local taverns and consorting with unsuitable women.

Long Millgate stank from the River Irk which had become an open sewer. The boys were expected to play in the street in front of taverns, warehouses and second rate undertakers. It would unfortunately take many years to resolve the School's accommodation problems.

The appointment of Frederick William Walker known as 'Malleus philosophorum' - the hammer of the philosophers - as High Master in 1859 with his stern emphasis on academic attainment led initially to a falling off of pupil numbers.

Word however eventually got around that despite its insalubrious surroundings, uncompromising academic excellence could be found at The Manchester Grammar School. By 1873 the School had 500 pupils and just three years later 750.

In 1868 the School had bought more land in Long Millgate for £1,000 and in 1871 took over a new building which had cost £28,000. By October 1880 a gymnasium costing £40,000 had also been added to the School's property. Further building in 1913 transformed narrow Long Millgate into a spacious quadrangle.

It was not enough: in September 1931 at a cost of £240,000 the whole school moved to a new site at Fallowfield, a brick subdued neo-

Georgian building. A new and incredibly short school day, 9.30 am to 3.45 pm, was instituted to accommodate day boys travelling from far and wide. The Fallowfield site bears witness to many more improvements with £4.5 million spent on new buildings in the 1990s. The new buildings included an English Centre; two language laboratories; an indoor swimming pool; a gymnasium; squash courts; separate junior and senior libraries; a theatre and lecture theatre; a careers room, a bookshop, run by the pupils themselves; two computer laboratories; 19 science laboratories; Art & Design studios; Music School; Sixth Form Common Rooms and a new Sports Hall.

Around 200 new pupils from 550 applicants are admitted to the student roll each year. Pupils are drawn from every kind of background, many taking advantage of the numerous bursaries available to help towards the cost of attending this foremost independent school. The School has successfully blended the focus upon scholarship central to High Master Walker's philosophy, with the passion for the education of the whole person so evident in the thinking of J G Paton, High Master from 1962 to 1978.

The outstanding academic strength of the School is balanced by a rich extra-curricular programme offering a cornucopia of choice to boys whilst some boys go on to achieve national and international success, many more get involved simply for fun, as well as for personal development.

As the School approaches its five hundredth birthday it can look forward to its second half millennium with confidence that it will continue to live up to its motto Sapere Aude, daring its pupils to be wise.

*Top left: Alderley Park Camp, 1904. **Top right:** The Queen on her visit to the school in 1965. **Left:** The Manchester Grammar School, 2006.*

Kellogg's - A Century of Breakfasts

There are only a handful of brand names which are instantly familiar throughout the whole world. One name which has membership of that elite club is Kellogg's.

Kellogg's celebrated its 100th anniversary in 2006. Centenary packs of Corn Flakes were produced which included a promotion to collect a gold heritage Kellogg's van.

The Kellogg's company built its first UK manufacturing plant at Trafford Park, Manchester in 1938. The world's largest cereal manufacturing plant, it was opened by Mansfield housewife, Mrs Florence Millward.

But what were the origins of Kellogg's? Though Kellogg's cereals are as ingrained in British breakfast culture as a nice cup of tea, the company had its beginnings in Michigan in the USA.

Cornflakes were invented by Will Keith Kellogg and his brother Dr John Harvey Kellogg, chief physician at Battle Creek's Medical and Surgical 'Sanatarium'.

Will Kellogg was bookkeeper at the health resort. He assisted his brother in research aimed at improving the diet of the Sanatarium's patients.

In 1894 Will Kellogg accidentally left a pot of boiled wheat to stand. When it was put through the usual rolling process each grain emerged as a large, thin flake. It looked like a culinary disaster, but baked and served

to patients the flakes were an immediate success.

Soon the flakes were being packaged by the Kellogg brothers' 'Sanitas Food Company' to meet mail order requests from former patients. Will, whose signature still adorns Kellogg's cereal packets, devoted the rest of his life to the breakfast cereal business founding the Battle Creek Toasted Corn Flake Company on 19th February 1906. Brother John by contrast concentrated on his medical career.

The company was re-named The Kellogg Company in 1922: two years later it began exporting Kellogg's Corn Flakes and Kellogg's All-Bran cereals to the United Kingdom.

As the business flourished, Kellogg's established the Kellogg Company of Great Britain, with offices in London, and set about establishing a national distribution network. At first the products sold in the UK were shipped from Canada and sold by a sales force supported by unemployed men and boy scouts.

Kellogg's Rice Krispies were introduced into the UK in 1928.

By 1936 Kellogg's UK sales topped £1million – with Kellogg's Corn Flakes priced at 5 old pennies a pack this equated to more than 50 million packets sold, one for every man woman and child in the country.

Top: *Kellogg's Cornflakes from 1938.*
Above left: *Advertising from the 1950s.*
Above: *Kellogg's Cornflakes with free Spinzip, 1959.*

Two years later, with war on the horizon, the company opened its plant in Manchester's Trafford Park. Though the plant would continue to operate through the war years production changed due to the scarcity of imported grains. For several years production of Kellogg's Corn Flakes and Kellogg's Rice Krispies ceased and the plant moved to the production of Wheat Flakes using homegrown wheat.

Company founder Will Kellogg died in 1951 at the age of 91. By then Britain's years of post-war austerity were coming to a close. New Kellogg's breakfast brands soon began to appear on grocers' shelves: Bran Flakes in 1952, and Frosties in 1954. The following year Kellogg's Rice Krispies put some snap crackle and pop into the rapidly recovering economy by adopting that famous slogan to promote that ever-popular product.

Kellogg's ran it's first on-pack promotion on Corn Flakes, called the Great Teaspoon collection, in 1957. With over half a million orders for the teaspoons the promotion was heavily over-subscribed and for that year made Kellogg's the biggest cutlery retailer in the UK. Later that same year thousands of small boys

begged their mothers to buy Kellogg's Corn Flakes in order that they could get their hands on the must-have giveaway plastic 'Atomic' submarine toy.

By 1964 Manchester had become only the second Kellogg's plant after Battle Creek to produce one million pounds of cereals in a day.

The original 'K' sign was commissioned for the Manchester plant in 1966 – at the time it was the largest illuminated letter in the country, at 45ft top to bottom.

The famous sign would remain a local landmark until 2004 when Tony the Tiger and Cornelius the Cockerel finally replaced the giant illumination.

Today the UK cereal industry is worth £1.43 billion: Kellogg's manufactures seven of the top ten selling cereal brands. A remark-able outcome for a company whose origins lie in a kitchen catastrophe!

Top: Rice Krispies, produced in 1927 and introduced to the UK in 1928, pictured is a cereal pack from 1960.
Left: Kellogg's Frosties and the famous Tony the Tiger from 1969.

Tenmat - A prize winning name

Getting a company's name right is important. And these days companies seem to change their names even more frequently than in the past in order to best reflect their current business focus.

Manchester based Tenmat Ltd's long evolution since the 1920s has resulted in several name changes along the way.

Today Tenmat is a leading manufacturer of specialised, high performance, non-metallic composite engineering materials and components supplied to a broad cross section of industrial applications throughout the world. The company has extensive in-house technical resources, and using these in conjunction with unrivalled innovation and technical expertise is consistently developing industry standard products.

The company's headquarters is situated in Trafford Park, Manchester where the first composite engineering components were created at the turn of the twentieth century. Tenmat also has facilities in Cradley Heath in the Midlands.

A decision to rename the company from TAC Engineering Materials to Tenmat was made in 1986, the prize winning suggestion made by the company painter who suggested it as an acronym of Turners Engineering Materials

The company can be traced back to 1920 when four existing companies, with histories of their own going back to the Victorian era, merged.

Top: Sir Samuel Turner, Chairman 1920-1924 and FS Newall Chairman 1924-1929. Below: Trafford Park Works, 1914.

building materials of all kinds seldom slackened. One of the largest projects in this period would be the cement roofing of the new Ocean Terminal at Southampton, over a quarter of a mile in length and designed for the reception of the Atlantic Queens, the great liners which then carried the bulk of trans-Atlantic passenger traffic.

Until 1986 the company's predominant products remained fibre and cement building and insulation products – using sheet-forming machines, presses, papermaking equipment and a resin impregnator.

The Turner Brothers Company, The Washington Chemical Company, the Newalls Insulation Company and JW Roberts Ltd joined forces to form Turner & Newall Ltd.

Turner Brothers, founded in 1871 had been operating at Trafford Park since 1914 and this would form a key component of the new company.

Fibre cement building sheets and roofing tiles were in great demand for many decades. 'Trafford Tile' was used extensively to roof the main hall at the Wembley Exhibition in 1924. The 'Big Six' corrugated sheet would go on to cover a greater area of industrial buildings than any other material in history.

In 1927 fibre cement pressure pipes were introduced for underground water mains and were sold throughout the world: in 1946 some 80 miles of such piping would be laid across the desert in schemes to provide both Mecca and Jeddah in Saudi Arabia with water.

The years of the second world war began with the company receiving huge orders to supply the slates and sheeting used to construct innumerable army camps, aerodrome hangars, stores, temporary hospitals and countless other wartime buildings.

Though the Trafford Park plant suffered from German bombing, production was not long interrupted as it workers struggled to do their bit.

Nor, unlike in the aftermath of the first world war, did demand fall off in the immediate post-war years. Bomb damage to both industrial and domestic property throughout Britain had been so extensive that demand for

Since then the company has converted to a new range of products, over half of which are exported around the world. Products are used for fire protection, 'arc chute' refurbishment, rotor vanes for vacuum pumps and compressors, in the aerospace industry, as well as in marine products, hydro-electric power stations the chemical industry and the railways.

In 1997 Tenmat was acquired in a Management buy-out led by its MD Tony Moore.

The Tenmat group now includes businesses in the USA, Germany, France and Italy as well as a global network of vendors and distributors.

Today Tenmat employs more than 180 staff at its Trafford Park HQ. Product testing and development is carried out in the R&D laboratory. The company's commitment to technical excellence in the supply of products for applications as diverse as furnace insulation and critical components for the aerospace industry has demanded a heavy investment in ongoing research and development to both extend the performance characteristics of existing product ranges and to take the company forward into totally new areas such as advanced 21st Century ceramics and composites.

Top: Segment punching for electric motors.
Right: Tenmat premises, 2006.

R H Lord & Son - Their name is spreading

Got an asphalting job needs doing? Then the place to enquire is R H Lord & Son (Asphalters) Ltd in Light Oaks Road, Salford – a family firm that's been in the business for over a century.

In the 1880s Ralph Herbert Lord was an international prize-winning photographer living in Cambridge. He was asked by his brother, then running his own asphalting business in Salford, to join him as a Director.

Unhappily the directorship never materialised. Instead, in 1890, Ralph set up his own business. He and his family moved to Mount Vernon, Eccles New Road, Salford from where Ralph and his second son, Herbert William, ran the firm.

Mastic asphalt is a waterproof material used on flat roofs or on floors, and for waterproofing underground rooms. Back then it was also used for roads, before the widespread use of tarmac. A lot of the work in those days was on mill roofs which were sometimes used as water tanks and therefore had to be watertight.

Asphalt is stored in block form and has to be melted and mixed using a boiler, which in those early days was coke-fired. The original boilers were horse–drawn, and the action of the horse in transit turned paddles in the boiler to mix the melting asphalt ready for use. Asphalt is hand-laid using wooden floats similar in size to plasterers' floats.

Business founder Ralph Lord died in 1922; Herbert's son, Bernard Hopewell Lord, now came into the business. He started out at the bottom, and would tell of the times when, working as a labourer, he kept his boiled egg warm by putting it in a billycan of freshly brewed tea.

Progress was in the offing. The firm now acquired a yard to house its boilers. In 1931 the firm became a limited company, which Bernard would run single-handed until his death in 1980.

Above left: Founder Ralph Herbert Lord.
Above right: Herbert William Lord.
Left: Asphalt being hand-laid using wooden floats similar in size to plasterers' floats.
Below: The original horse–drawn boiler.

the company to work out the three months notice due to the employees. Hazel had always been interested in the company but had not had any experience; happily she had the expertise and loyalty of the staff to enable her to succeed.

At this point Hazel's son Mark Robert Ashley Sandiford, then doing his O Levels, expressed an interest in eventually working in the firm. Hazel kept the business going during Mark's absence at University. After Mark graduated they worked together for three years before he took over in 1989.

As the building trade was a reserved occupation during the 1939-45 war the firm carried on, and was necessarily kept busy. Boilers were now towed by lorries. The firm's car which Bernard had used to supervise work sites was put up on blocks in the yard until 1947: Bernard had to go out with the lorry driver until the firm was allowed a van using rationed 'red' petrol when the boilers were left on site.

During this time Bernard began to manufacture his own blocks using the horse-drawn boilers which had been converted to use electricity.

The firm was at its largest during Bernard's tenure; and by the late 1960s was employing 38 men. Although there was still work done on cotton mills in the 1960s a lot of work was being done on multi-storey blocks of flats built by local authorities. As Bernard got older however he reduced the workforce in anticipation of his retirement and of the firm closing. By the time of his death at the age of 76 Bernard was employing only five long-serving men whom he had no wish to put out of work.

Bernard died very suddenly, and at that point his daughter Vera Hazel Sandiford discovered that she was a director and took over

Until the 1950s the asphalt used was Natural Rock Asphalt occurring naturally in asphalt lakes in Trinidad & Tobago and a number of other places. That is now so expensive that it is rarely used. Natural asphalt is the residue left from reservoirs of crude oil evaporating over millions of years – today's asphalt is manufactured using bitumen and aggregates.

Though it may not have yet racked up a million years in business R H Lord & Son (Asphalters) Ltd's high standards and quality of service have enabled it to become not only the oldest asphalting company in Manchester but quite possibly in the whole of Britain.

Top left: Bernard Hopewell Lord.
Below left: Vera Hazel Sandiford.
Above: Mark Robert Ashley Sandiford.
Below: The company's current boilers.

ACKNOWLEDGMENTS

The publishers would like to thank

Manchester Central Library: Local Studies Unit

Andrew Mitchell

Steve Ainsworth

All reasonable steps were taken by the publishers of this book to trace the copyright holders and obtain permission to use the photographs contained herein. However, due to the passage of time certain individuals were untraceable. Should any interested party subsequently come to light, the publishers can be contacted at the phone number printed at the front of this book and the appropriate arrangements will then be made.

Memories of Accrington - 1 903204 05 4

Memories of Barnet - 1 903204 16 X

Memories of Barnsley - 1 900463 11 3

More Memories of Barnsley - 1 903 204 79 8

Golden Years of Barnsley -1 900463 87 3

Memories of Basingstoke - 1 903204 26 7

Memories of Bedford - 1 900463 83 0

More Memories of Bedford - 1 903204 33 X

Golden Years of Birmingham - 1 900463 04 0

Birmingham Memories - 1 903204 45 3

More Birmingham Memories - 1 903204 80 1

Memories of Blackburn - 1 900463 40 7

More Memories of Blackburn - 1 900463 96 2

Memories of Blackpool - 1 900463 21 0

Memories of Bolton - 1 900463 45 8

More Memories of Bolton - 1 900463 13 X

Bolton Memories - 1 903204 37 2

Memories of Bournemouth -1 900463 44 X

Memories of Bradford - 1 900463 00 8

More Memories of Bradford - 1 900463 16 4

More Memories of Bradford II - 1 900463 63 6

Bradford Memories - 1 903204 47 X

Bradford City Memories - 1 900463 57 1

Memories of Bristol - 1 900463 78 4

More Memories of Bristol - 1 903204 43 7

Memories of Bromley - 1 903204 21 6

Memories of Burnley - 1 900463 95 4

Golden Years of Burnley - 1 900463 67 9

Memories of Bury - 1 900463 90 3

More Memories of Bury - 1 903 204 78 X

Memories of Cambridge - 1 900463 88 1

Memories of Cardiff - 1 900463 14 8

More Memories of Cardiff - 1 903204 73 9

Memories of Carlisle - 1 900463 38 5

Memories of Chelmsford - 1 903204 29 1

Memories of Cheltenham - 1 903204 17 8

Memories of Chester - 1 900463 46 6

More Memories of Chester -1 903204 02 X

Chester Memories - 1 903204 83 6

Memories of Chesterfield -1 900463 61 X

More Memories of Chesterfield - 1 903204 28 3

Memories of Colchester - 1 900463 74 1

Nostalgic Coventry - 1 900463 58 X

Coventry Memories - 1 903204 38 0

Memories of Croydon - 1 900463 19 9

More Memories of Croydon - 1 903204 35 6

Golden Years of Darlington - 1 900463 72 5

Nostalgic Darlington - 1 900463 31 8

Darlington Memories - 1 903204 46 1

Memories of Derby - 1 900463 37 7

More Memories of Derby - 1 903204 20 8

Memories of Dewsbury & Batley - 1 900463 80 6

Memories of Doncaster - 1 900463 36 9

More Memories of Doncaster - 1 903204 75 5

Nostalgic Dudley - 1 900463 03 2

Golden Years of Dudley - 1 903204 60 7

Memories of Edinburgh - 1 900463 33 4

More memories of Edinburgh - 1903204 72 0

Memories of Enfield - 1 903204 14 3

Memories of Exeter - 1 900463 94 6

Memories of Glasgow - 1 900463 68 7

More Memories of Glasgow - 1 903204 44 5

Memories of Gloucester - 1 903204 04 6

Memories of Grimsby - 1 900463 97 0

More Memories of Grimsby - 1 903204 36 4

Memories of Guildford - 1 903204 22 4

Memories of Halifax - 1 900463 05 9

More Memories of Halifax - 1 900463 06 7

Golden Years of Halifax - 1 900463 62 8

Nostalgic Halifax - 1 903204 30 5

Memories of Harrogate - 1 903204 01 1

Memories of Hartlepool - 1 900463 42 3

Memories of High Wycombe - 1 900463 84 9

Memories of Huddersfield - 1 900463 15 6

More Memories of Huddersfield - 1 900463 26 1

Golden Years of Huddersfield - 1 900463 77 6

Nostalgic Huddersfield - 1 903204 19 4

Huddersfield Memories - 1903204 86 0

Huddersfield Town FC - 1 900463 51 2

Memories of Hull - 1 900463 86 5

More Memories of Hull - 1 903204 06 2

Hull Memories - 1 903204 70 4

True North Books Ltd - Book List

Memories of Keighley - 1 900463 01 6

Golden Years of Keighley - 1 900463 92 X

Memories of Kingston - 1 903204 24 0

Memories of Leeds - 1 900463 75 X

More Memories of Leeds - 1 900463 12 1

Golden Years of Leeds - 1 903204 07 0

Memories of Leicester - 1 900463 08 3

Leeds Memories - 1 903204 62 3

More Memories of Leicester - 1 903204 08 9

Memories of Leigh - 1 903204 27 5

Memories of Lincoln - 1 900463 43 1

Memories of Liverpool - 1 900463 07 5

More Memories of Liverpool - 1 903204 09 7

Liverpool Memories - 1 903204 53 4

More Liverpool Memories - 1 903204 88 7

Memories of Luton - 1 900463 93 8

Memories of Macclesfield - 1 900463 28 8

Memories of Manchester - 1 900463 27 X

More Memories of Manchester - 1 903204 03 8

Manchester Memories - 1 903204 54 2

More Manchester Memories - 1 903204 89 5

Memories of Middlesbrough - 1 900463 56 3

More Memories of Middlesbrough - 1 903204 42 9

Memories of Newbury - 1 900463 79 2

Memories of Newcastle - 1 900463 81 4

More Memories of Newcastle - 1 903204 10 0

Newcastle Memories - 1.903204 71 2

Memories of Newport - 1 900463 59 8

Memories of Northampton - 1 900463 48 2

More Memories of Northampton - 1 903204 34 8

Memories of Norwich - 1 900463 73 3

Memories of Nottingham - 1 900463 91 1

More Memories of Nottingham - 1 903204 11 9

Nottingham Memories - 1 903204 63 1

Bygone Oldham - 1 900463 25 3

Memories of Oldham - 1 900463 76 8

More Memories of Oldham - 1 903204 84 4

Memories of Oxford - 1 900463 54 7

Memories of Peterborough - 1 900463 98 9

Golden Years of Poole - 1 900463 69 5

Memories of Portsmouth - 1 900463 39 3

More Memories of Portsmouth - 1 903204 51 8

Nostalgic Preston - 1 900463 50 4

More Memories of Preston - 1 900463 17 2

Preston Memories - 1 903204 41 0

Memories of Reading - 1 900463 49 0

Memories of Rochdale - 1 900463 60 1

More Memories of Reading - 1 903204 39 9

More Memories of Rochdale - 1 900463 22 9

Memories of Romford - 1 903204 40 2

Memories of Rothertham- 1903204 77 1

Memories of St Albans - 1 903204 23 2

Memories of St Helens - 1 900463 52 0

Memories of Sheffield - 1 900463 20 2

More Memories of Sheffield - 1 900463 32 6

Golden Years of Sheffield - 1 903204 13 5

Memories of Slough - 1 900 463 29 6

Golden Years of Solihull - 1 903204 55 0

Memories of Southampton - 1 900463 34 2

More Memories of Southampton - 1 903204 49 6

Memories of Stockport - 1 900463 55 5

More Memories of Stockport - 1 903204 18 6

Stockport Memories - 1 903204 87 9

Memories of Stockton - 1 900463 41 5

Memories of Stoke-on-Trent - 1 900463 47 4

More Memories of Stoke-on-Trent - 1 903204 12 7

Memories of Stourbridge - 1903204 31 3

Memories of Sunderland - 1 900463 71 7

More Memories of Sunderland - 1 903204 48 8

Memories of Swindon - 1 903204 00 3

Memories of Uxbridge - 1 900463 64 4

Memories of Wakefield - 1 900463 65 2

More Memories of Wakefield - 1 900463 89 X

Nostalgic Walsall - 1 900463 18 0

Golden Years of Walsall - 1 903204 56 9

More Memories of Warrington - 1 900463 02 4

Warrington Memories - 1 903204 85 2

Memories of Watford - 1 900463 24 5

Golden Years of West Bromwich - 1 900463 99 7

Memories of Wigan - 1 900463 85 7

Golden Years of Wigan - 1 900463 82 2

More Memories of Wigan - 1 903204 82 8

Nostalgic Wirral - 1 903204 15 1

Wirral Memories - 1 903204 747

Memories of Woking - 1 903204 32 1

Nostalgic Wolverhampton - 1 900463 53 9

Wolverhampton Memories - 1 903204 50 X

Memories of Worcester - 1 903204 25 9

Memories of Wrexham - 1 900463 23 7

Memories of York - 1 900463 66 0